COMPETITORS

ADRIAN **BUCHAN**	JEREMY **FLORES****	JORDY **SMITH**†	OWEN **WRIGHT**	BEDE **DURBIDGE**	MICHEL **BOUREZ***
CHRIS **DAVIDSON**	JADSON **ANDRE**	RAONI **MONTEIRO***	HEITOR **ALVES**	ALEJO **MUNIZ**	KIEREN **PERROW**
CORY **LOPEZ**	TRAVIS **LOGIE**†	RICARDO **DOS SANTOS**	KAI **OTTON***	TAYLOR **KNOX**	DUSTY **PAYNE**†
TAJ **BURROW**	MICK **FANNING**	KELLY **SLATER**	JOEL **PARKINSON**	DAMIEN **HOBGOOD**	ADRIANO **DE SOUZA**
MATT **WILKINSON****	TIAGO **PIRES**	DANIEL **ROSS**	CJ **HOBGOOD**	PATRICK **GUDAUSKAS**	JULIAN **WILSON**
FREDRICK **PATACCHIA**	GABE **KLING**	HEIARII **WILLIAMS**†	ADAM **MELLING**	BRETT **SIMPSON**	JOSH **KERR**

{ *SCORED A 10 ... † INJURED IN ACTION }

CHARGERS

BRUCE **IRONS**	DAVE **RASTOVICH**	THIERRY **DOMENECH**	KAIMANA **ALEXANDER**	RODRIGO **KOXA**	ALEX **GRAY**
NATHAN **FLETCHER**	EVERALDO **PATO**	PEDRO **VIANA**	ADAM **ESPOSITO**	CARLOS **BURLE**	SEAN **LOPEZ**
DYLAN **LONGBOTTOM**	**GORDO**	KEALA **KENNELLY**	MAKUA **ROTHMAN**	RAIMANA **VAN BASTOLAER**	DEAN **MORRISON**
DEAN **BOWEN**	**MANU**	FRED **PATACCHIA**	LAURIE **TOWNER**	RYAN **HIPWOOD**	BRUNO **SANTOS**
KOBY **ABBERTON**	NICOLAS **LEETHAM**	MAYA **GABEIRA**	FELIPE **CESARANO**	STRIDER **WASILEWSKI**	
KALANI **CHAPMAN**	VETEA **DAVID**	JULIAN **WILSON**	BENJAMIN **SANCHEZ**	ANTHONY **WALSH**	

OUR STORY STARTS IN CLOUDS

WITH A MILLION YEARS OF
RAINWATER RETURNING
ITSELF TO THE PACIFIC

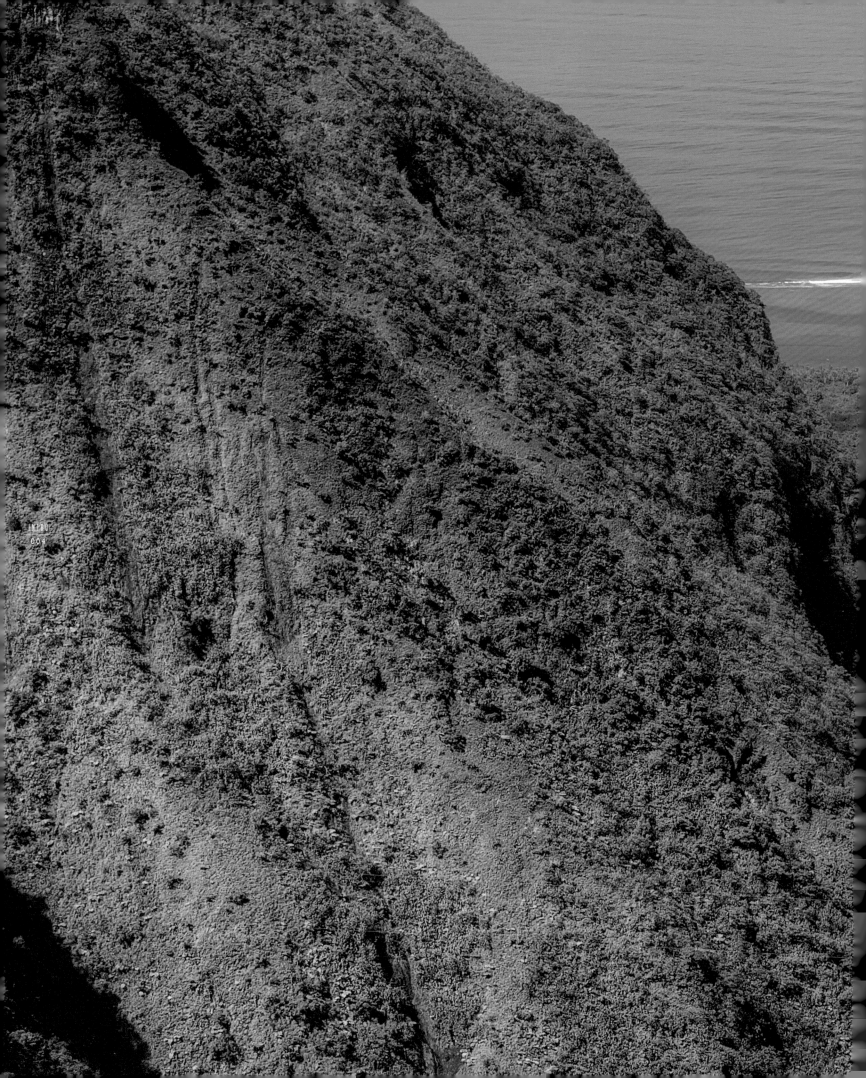

THE STREAMS FORMED A RIVER

AND THE RIVER FORGED A VALLEY

THE VALLEY BECAME A HOME

AND THE RIVER BORE A PASS IN THE REEF

AND ALONG THE REEF'S EDGE

A WAVE WRAPS ALONG THE LINE
OF THAT FRESHWATER BLADE

IT'S A WAVE LIKE NO OTHER

A WAVE OF ASTONISHING BEAUTY AND POWER

TEAH

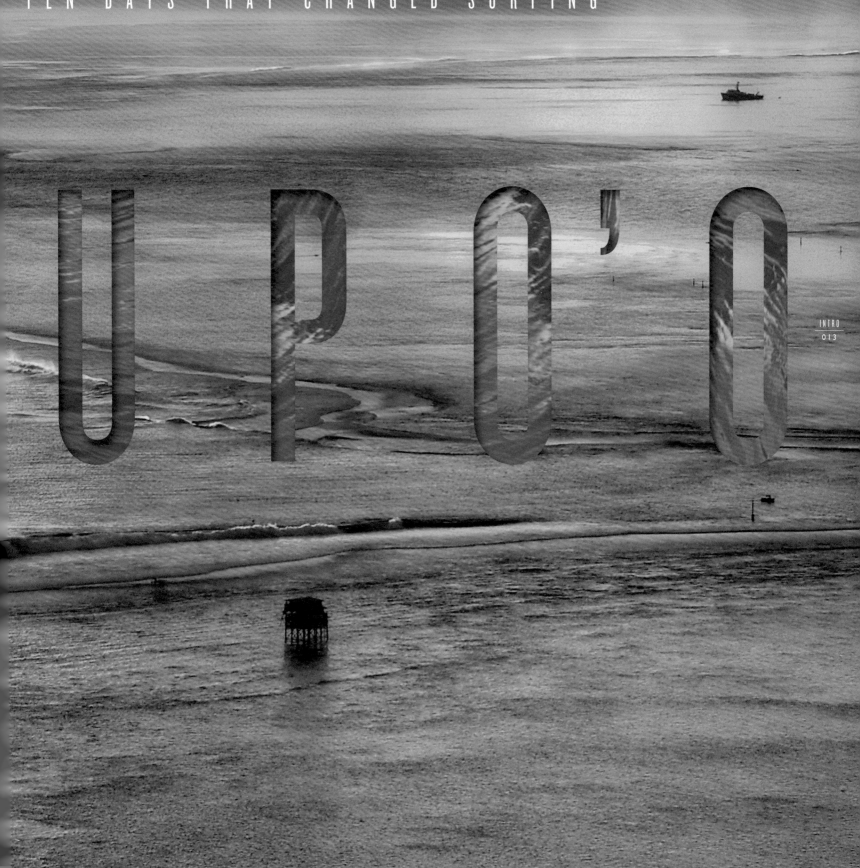

TEN DAYS THAT CHANGED SURFING

UPO'O

CONTENTS
014

016

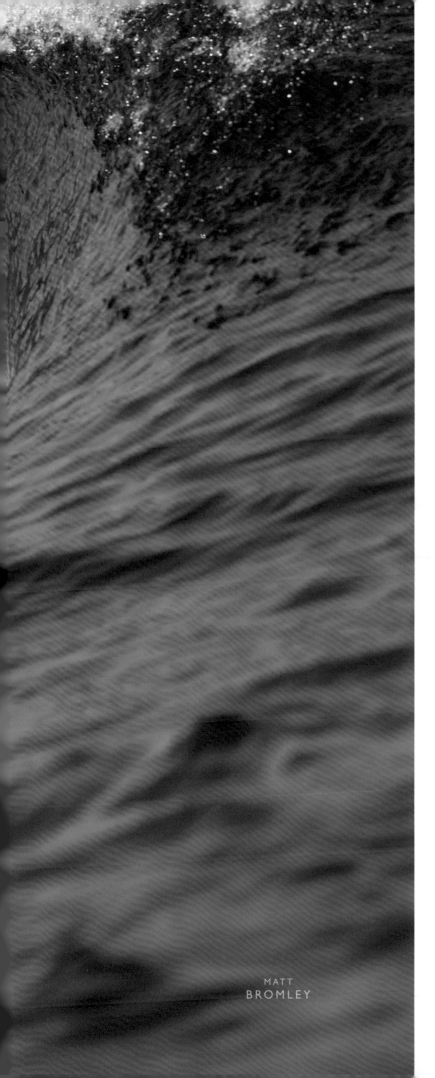

MATT
BROMLEY

IS IT REAL?

— 18/08/2011 —

GETTING SETTLED
INTO TEAHUPO'O
IS A BEAUTIFUL
CHALLENGE

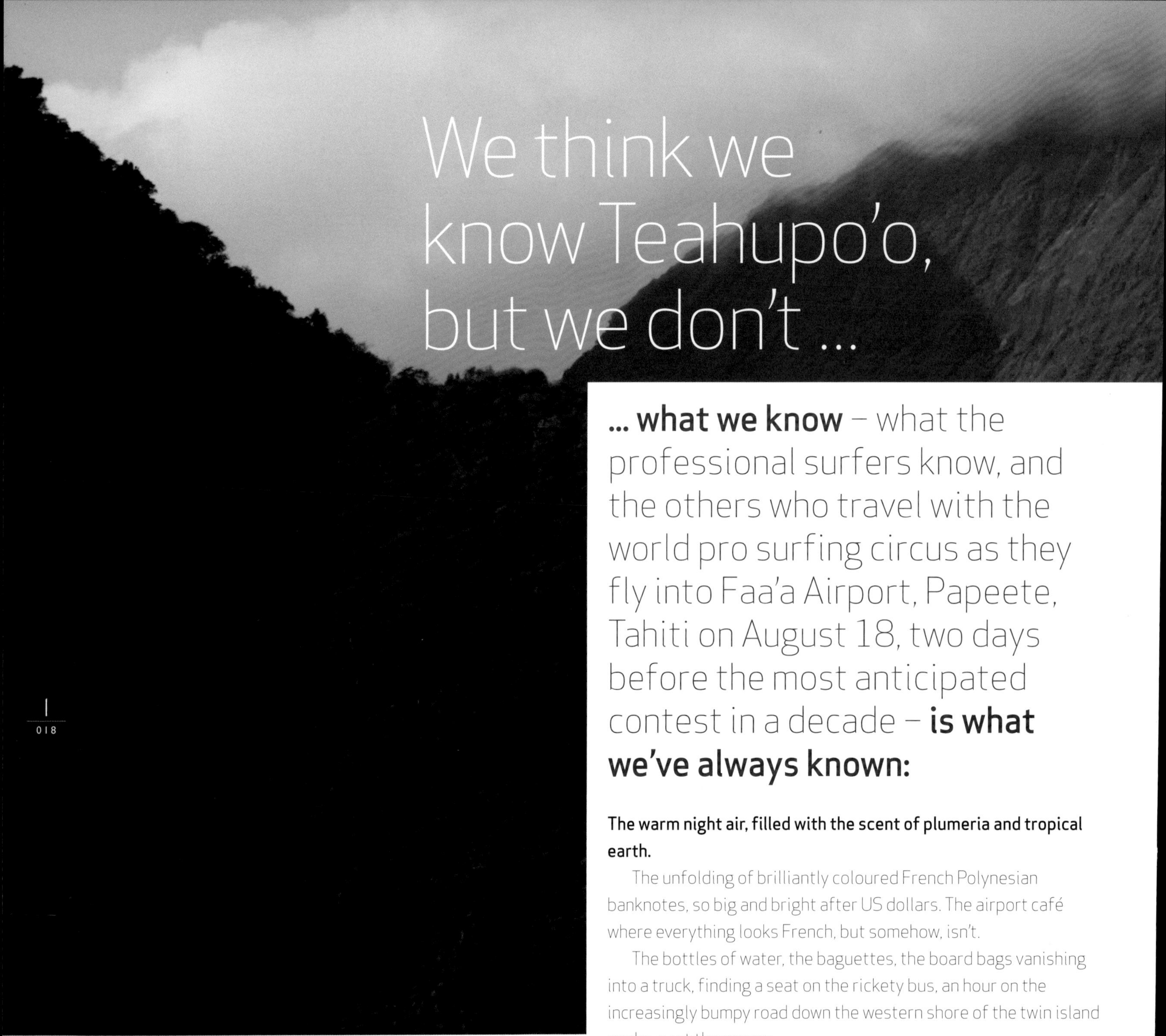

We think we know Teahupo'o, but we don't ...

... what we know – what the professional surfers know, and the others who travel with the world pro surfing circus as they fly into Faa'a Airport, Papeete, Tahiti on August 18, two days before the most anticipated contest in a decade – **is what we've always known:**

The warm night air, filled with the scent of plumeria and tropical earth.

The unfolding of brilliantly coloured French Polynesian banknotes, so big and bright after US dollars. The airport café where everything looks French, but somehow, isn't.

The bottles of water, the baguettes, the board bags vanishing into a truck, finding a seat on the rickety bus, an hour on the increasingly bumpy road down the western shore of the twin island peaks, past the names ...

... the names, Punaaiua, Taapuna, Sapinus, Maraa, Taiarapu, Taravao, Vairao, each drawing the mind to a memory of a matching wave out past the lagoon, unseen at midnight other than by brief glittering reflections of a sailing boat's mast-lights...

The conversations as people on the bus begin to relax into the night air's warmth and into each other's company again, into the shared awareness of another task, another event ahead of us.

But this is not another event. Far away, two thousand or more nautical miles to the south-west, the leading edge of a cold front is feeling its way into the ocean waters south of New Zealand. Behind it swells the first intimation of something the surf forecasters

have been warning about for over a week, the biggest and most powerful Southern Ocean storm of an already active winter season.

Everyone on the bus has heard about or seen this forecast, and they talk about it in snippets, short nervous sentences exchanged over the stutter of the bus's jangly engine and the roar of wind past its windows.

"Ever seen it big?"

"How big do you reckon?"

"Fifteen foot at 19 seconds!"

"What boards'd you bring?"

"I've left a 7'0" here for six years, might finally get to use it."

The forecast, and the last time Teahupo'o was big, and who was here back then in 2002 when Shane Powell pulled into that huge half-forgotten cavern, to be engraved on surf mag covers around the globe. Everyone laughs to recall that picture again – Shane clinging to hope just ahead of the foamball, before it swallowed him up and smashed him to half-drowning. A moment of glory that eventually sent him back to Avoca Beach then to fishing in Yamba.

2002, when a 23-year-old Phillip Andrew Irons ripped the covers off his freshly minted plans for a world pro surfing championship, winning on the massive days, winning the final in four-foot surf and a shower of champagne, on the way to being the biggest surf star on earth.

Then all the slow years in between – the waiting-period extensions, the weeks of nothing but trickly waves in the smaller passes, the dashes to finish before a three-foot swell disappeared, the drama and excitement of 2010 and Al's last win, the late, great Andy's last great moment.

The talk circles around, telling the stories and re-telling them, some of it half missed under the roar of the bus, people straining to hear.

"You saw that? I always wondered."

"Jeez it was boring, I'd already been here for three weeks and it never got over two foot."

"What was it? Andy's sending this swell?"

The headlights are beginning to catch kilometre stones by the roadside, little red and white streaks through the dark: Teahupoo 7. Teahupoo 3.

Then with a jolt as the bus's front wheels stop in a mud puddle under the last street light in southern Tahiti, we're there.

People stumble out, drag boardbags from the truck, sniff the warm air, listen to the quiet clanking of rock against rock in the rivermouth… disperse into the darkness, flashlights flickering, led away to their Tahitian host families.

Tomorrow we'll wake up in flower-print sheets to the cackling of roosters and the barking of dogs, and say hello to people we haven't seen in a year. Drink fresh coconut juice, wax up a small board and paddle out for a warmup. And in between the little three-footers – caught even at this size half-nervously, with eyes averted from the reef's razorblades beneath the silk of the water surface – we'll wonder if the forecast is really truly real.

It's been a strange year so far for professional surfing; the surf's been small, the schedule rearranged around big city events with plenty of zing but not much hope of waves. Could Teahupo'o the never-quite-epic be about to turn it around? Has Al's animal spirit lingered long enough to bless us at this, his all-time favourite spot?

But Teahupo'o itself will not even offer us a hint. Teahupo'o is not subject to human whim or belief. It's a 10,000-year-old reef pass in the middle of the Pacific Ocean and it will do whatever it will do. We thought we knew what that might be, but we don't. **Not yet.** ∎

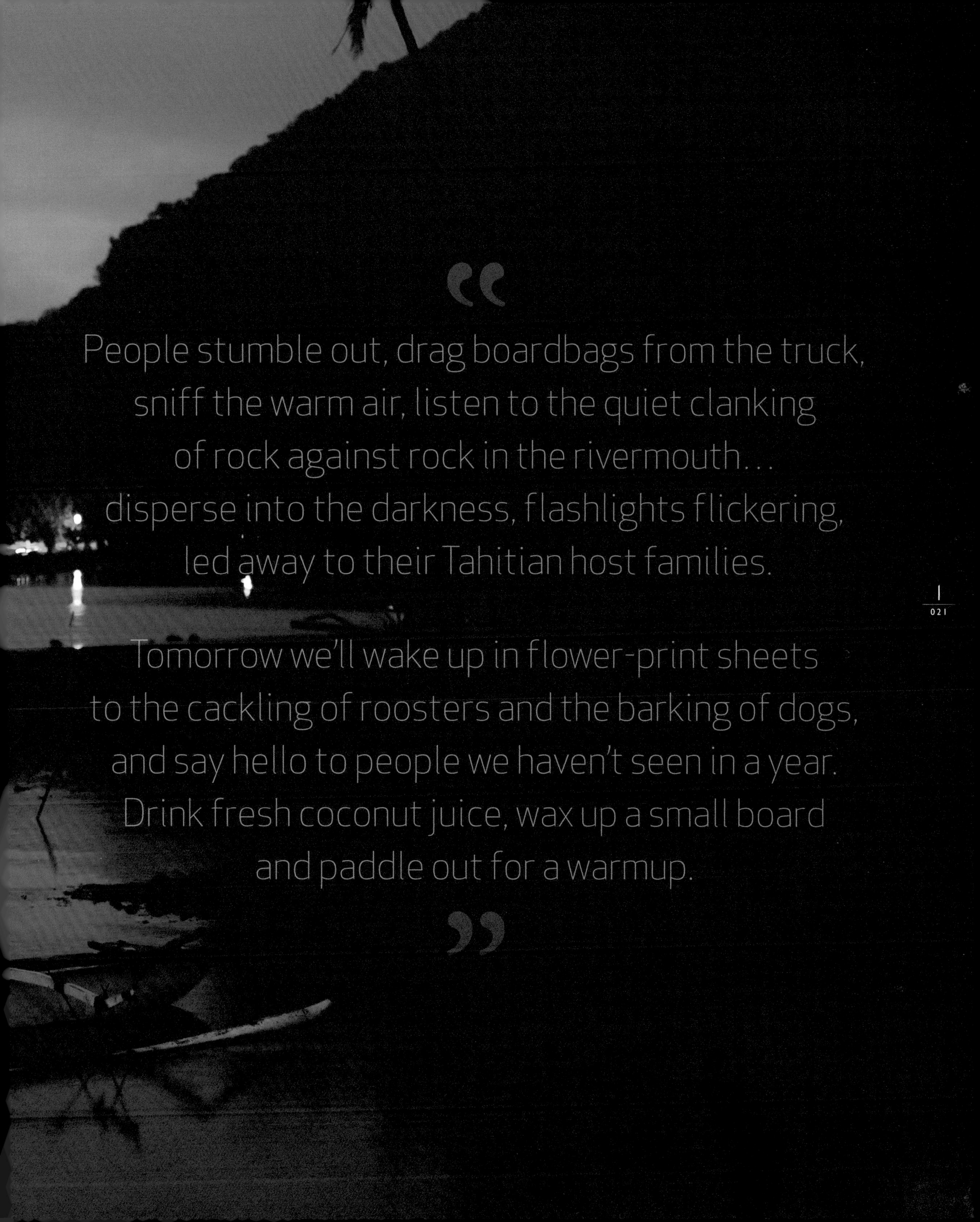

"

People stumble out, drag boardbags from the truck,
sniff the warm air, listen to the quiet clanking
of rock against rock in the rivermouth…
disperse into the darkness, flashlights flickering,
led away to their Tahitian host families.

Tomorrow we'll wake up in flower-print sheets
to the cackling of roosters and the barking of dogs,
and say hello to people we haven't seen in a year.
Drink fresh coconut juice, wax up a small board
and paddle out for a warmup.

"

022

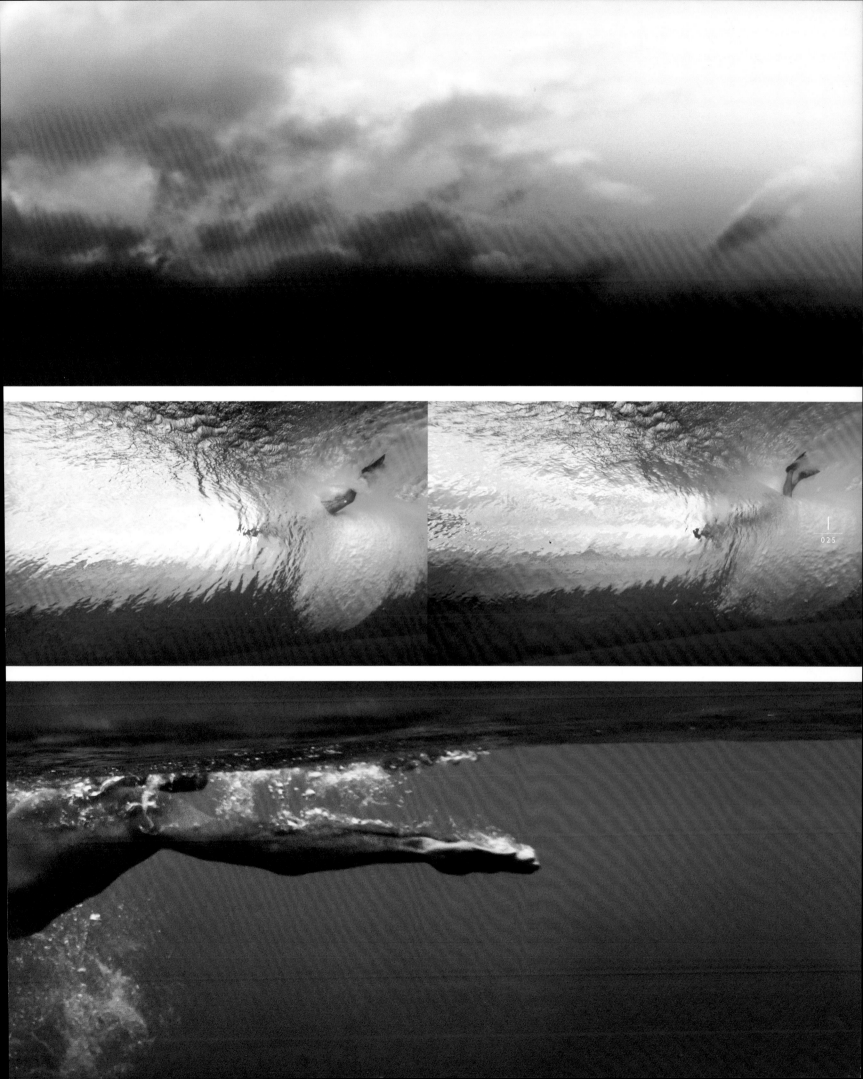

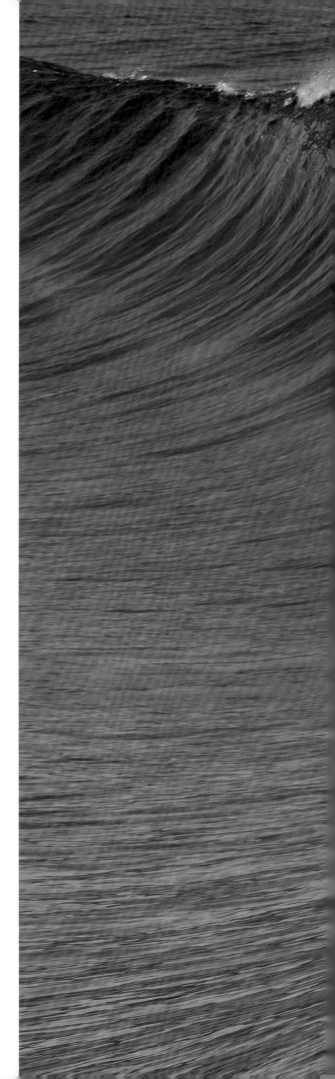

OWEN
WRIGHT

TAJ
BURROW

20/08/2011

ROUND ONE BUSINESS AND FREE SURF FUN AS THE ASTONISHING FORECAST LOOMS

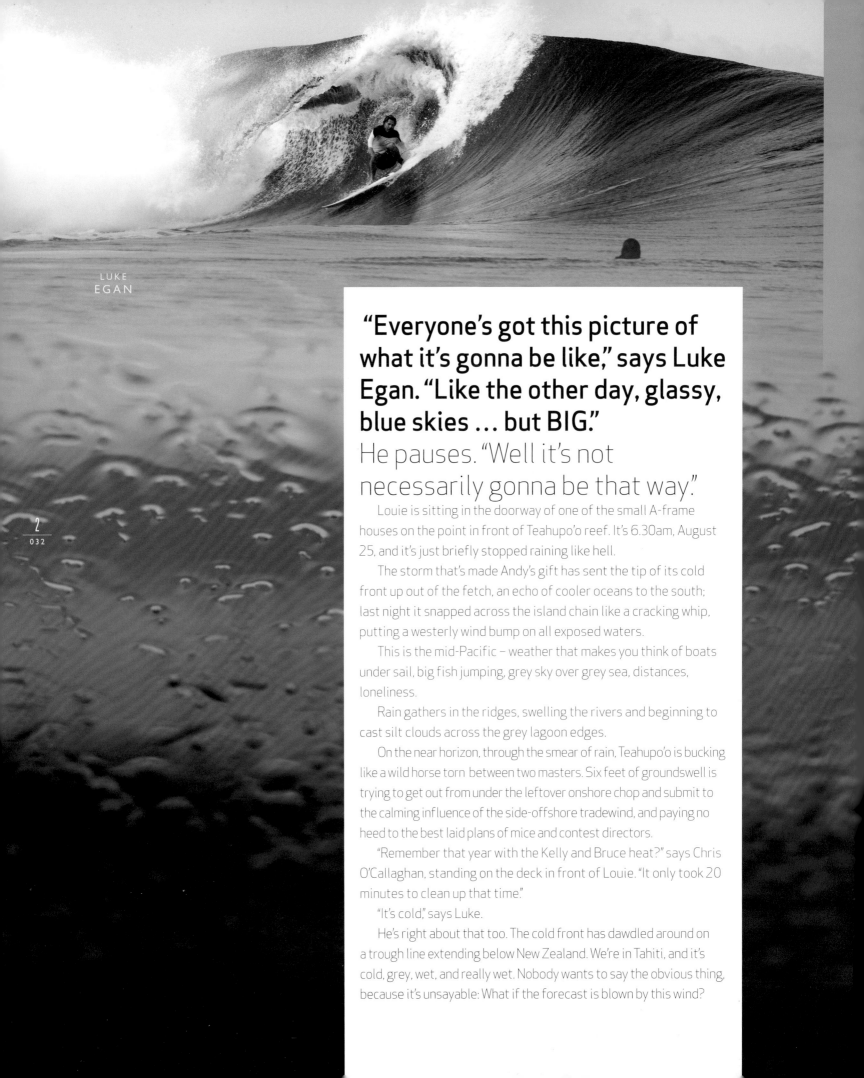

"Everyone's got this picture of what it's gonna be like," says Luke Egan. "Like the other day, glassy, blue skies … but BIG."

He pauses. "Well it's not necessarily gonna be that way."

Louie is sitting in the doorway of one of the small A-frame houses on the point in front of Teahupo'o reef. It's 6.30am, August 25, and it's just briefly stopped raining like hell.

The storm that's made Andy's gift has sent the tip of its cold front up out of the fetch, an echo of cooler oceans to the south; last night it snapped across the island chain like a cracking whip, putting a westerly wind bump on all exposed waters.

This is the mid-Pacific – weather that makes you think of boats under sail, big fish jumping, grey sky over grey sea, distances, loneliness.

Rain gathers in the ridges, swelling the rivers and beginning to cast silt clouds across the grey lagoon edges.

On the near horizon, through the smear of rain, Teahupo'o is bucking like a wild horse torn between two masters. Six feet of groundswell is trying to get out from under the leftover onshore chop and submit to the calming influence of the side-offshore tradewind, and paying no heed to the best laid plans of mice and contest directors.

"Remember that year with the Kelly and Bruce heat?" says Chris O'Callaghan, standing on the deck in front of Louie. "It only took 20 minutes to clean up that time."

"It's cold," says Luke.

He's right about that too. The cold front has dawdled around on a trough line extending below New Zealand. We're in Tahiti, and it's cold, grey, wet, and really wet. Nobody wants to say the obvious thing, because it's unsayable: What if the forecast is blown by this wind?

"The other day" Luke's mentioned, back on the 20th, the first day of competition, is cold too, at least at dawn. Tahiti can be chilly on a clear winter morning, as cool air from the mountaintops flows down into the valleys and pushes the ocean's warmth a little way offshore.

One result – as the cooler air settles on the water surface – is that characteristic dead calm of Teahupo'o's early hours; water like flattened silk, parting with a soft hiss under pressure of a boat hull or a rail turn. Sounds carry across the water: a barge loaded with judges meandering out to the tower, jetskis rushing surfers to the lineup, and always the crack of waves behind the reef line.

The evening before, they'd held the opening ceremony out on the point, and a blessing for Al with Teahupo'o spitting away in the background, and as Bruce Irons threw leis for his brother into the lagoon current and brushed away tears, the sense had grown stronger of how this year would indeed be different to last.

Back on the point, Dr Paul Fischer and his medical team have set up pro surfing's only dedicated emergency bay, complete with two resuscitation centres and fearsome trays of metallic instruments. He laughs when asked if the surfers want to check up on the medical prep: "They sorta want to avoid us. Because when we start talking about what we've got and what we're ready for, they get nervous."

But when the heats begin, it all goes to script, a classic four foot plus day, the sun warming the lagoon between occasional brief tradewind showers, a small crowd of boats gathering in the channel to watch. Playtime.

Every heat winner gets there in slightly different fashion: Freddy P by going hard, Travis Logie by being in the spot, Fanning by competitive skill, Jordy by force, Kelly by hard work, Kai Otton by a great first wave, Taylor Knox and Damien Hobgood by cool-headedness, Dusty and Julian by tube sense.

And CJ Hobgood by the lights of the Lord. CJ had scored three eights so far this whole year, but in this heat he throws away two eights to win with a 9.5 and a 9.8 – heat score of the year so far.

CJ's jolting score feels like a quick flash, a hint of what might be to come in the next five or six days, in which you can't help but wonder what other records might be broken. On the beach, everyone is talking about the swell – the one still somewhere over the horizon, the one some people are already calling at 15 to 20 feet, and other people still aren't sure is real.

O'Callaghan is relaxed about it. "Those days you see the tow guys getting those huge ones?" he says. "About five waves like that come through in the whole day. The tow teams hang around for three hours in between waiting for one."

Jordy asks CJ what to do if it comes down to that. "Well, you just get the in-between ones, and make sure you don't get caught inside!" laughs Ceej. "What else are you gonna do?"

By the time that wet, cold morning rolls around the forecast is irrelevant. The winds making Andy's gift have already done their work: a flat, broad, 800-nautical-mile fetch of 35-to-50-knot winds east of New Zealand's South Island, aimed clean at the Society Islands.

This storm and the one behind it will rip swell across the Pacific like a gigantic Gatling gun, hammering everywhere from Alaska to Peru, getting humans barrelled from Chicama to Barra de la Cruz … but first in the firing line will be here.

Chris Davidson and I decide what the hell, so what if it's a mess, get some wax on the feet. For a mad few minutes I think we might be the only ones out … but no. By the time we get to it, in the lineup is Dusty Payne, Ricardo dos Santos, Cory Lopez, Occ, Louie, Parko.

Teahupo'o is wobbling, surging and grinding. The wind is working on it, but that job is far from finished. Set waves are emerging from the chop outside the reef, swinging in, and gaining shape at the last second as the coral forces a clean curve from their bases. Six foot and bigger sets sucking back in on the reef, some sectioning, others reeling, a couple spitting.

It's beginning.

Parko snaps a board. Luke gets a bomb that sets up perfectly.

Occ gets a little beauty, paddles back out, sits, turns for another to find Ricardo paddling up his inside.

"Wonder why he does that?" says Cory dryly. "Wouldn't be anything geographical."

Cory Lopez is running this lineup. Cory is a wonderful and experienced surfer, but at Teahupo'o he becomes something more. He looks at waves with a flat, dark, fearless eye, judging them almost coldly, and when he makes a move for one, everyone leaves it alone.

"Scared," he says, "I'll be scared when it's big."

Dusty misses a solid one, just pulling back in time to stop himself from going over, then sits and waits for ages. Finally he gets a drainer, playing it cool on the paddle-in, and free-falls eight or 10 feet to the base, hitting flat water in full grab-rail stance with a jolt and almost recovering in time to make it, but being buried instead.

Late in the afternoon the wind dies and Dusty rides a clean wave all the way into the reef, falls through the silk on to the razorblade and rips his knee wide open. The docs clean the wound and insert 13 stitches. Dusty won't surf again for two weeks. He is just the first. ∎

MARK
OCCHILUPO

2
035

"

You'd think having 20 boats and 400 people staring at you across the lineup might be a bit distracting. And you'd be right. Until you take off and engage with the wave's intensity.

"

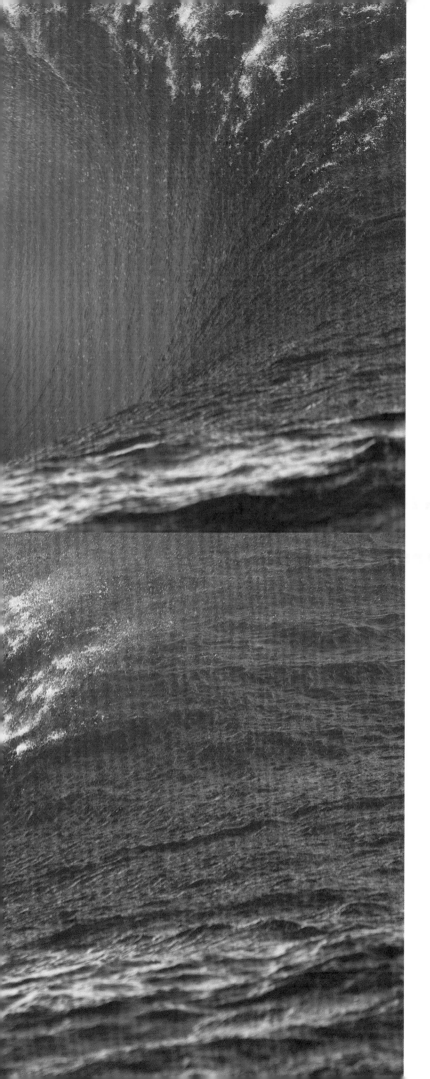

THE SN A R L

26/08/2011

BOMBS
DETONATE
AND WORLDS
COLLIDE

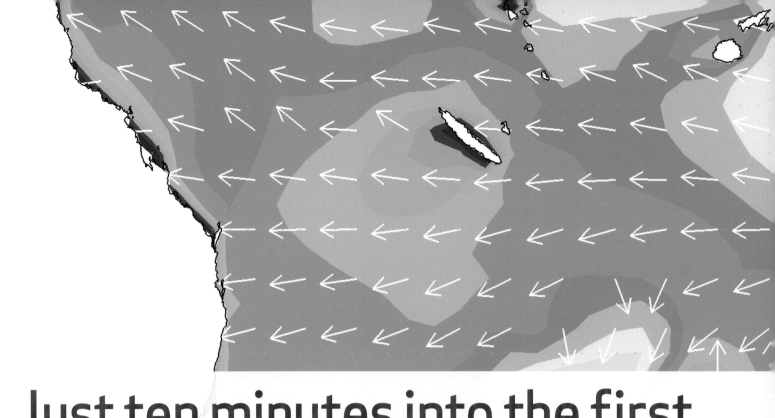

Just ten minutes into the first heat of August 26, Teahupo'o bares its teeth with a ten-foot set. The second wave of the set is not remotely rideable.

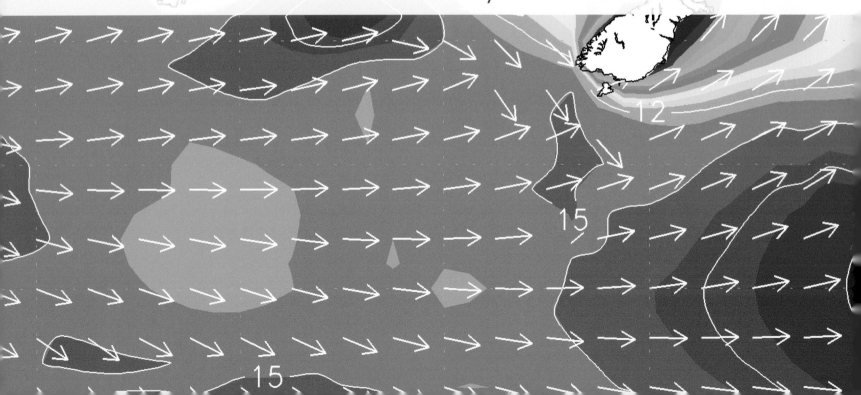

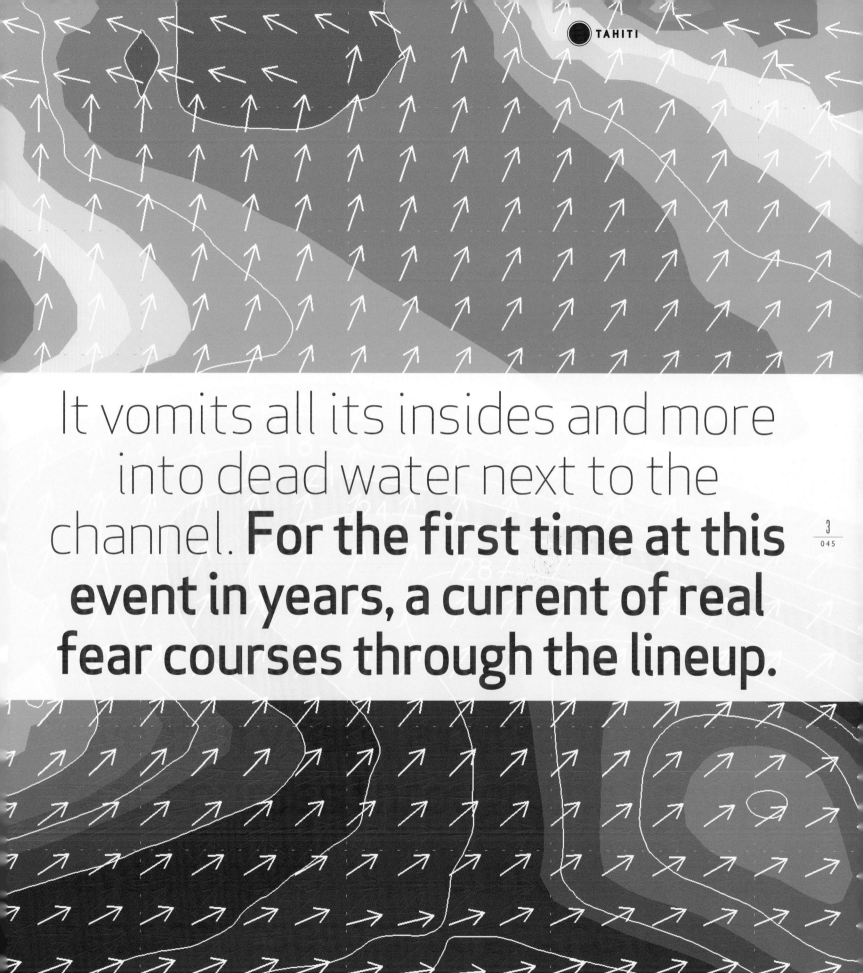

It vomits all its insides and more into dead water next to the channel. **For the first time at this event in years, a current of real fear courses through the lineup.**

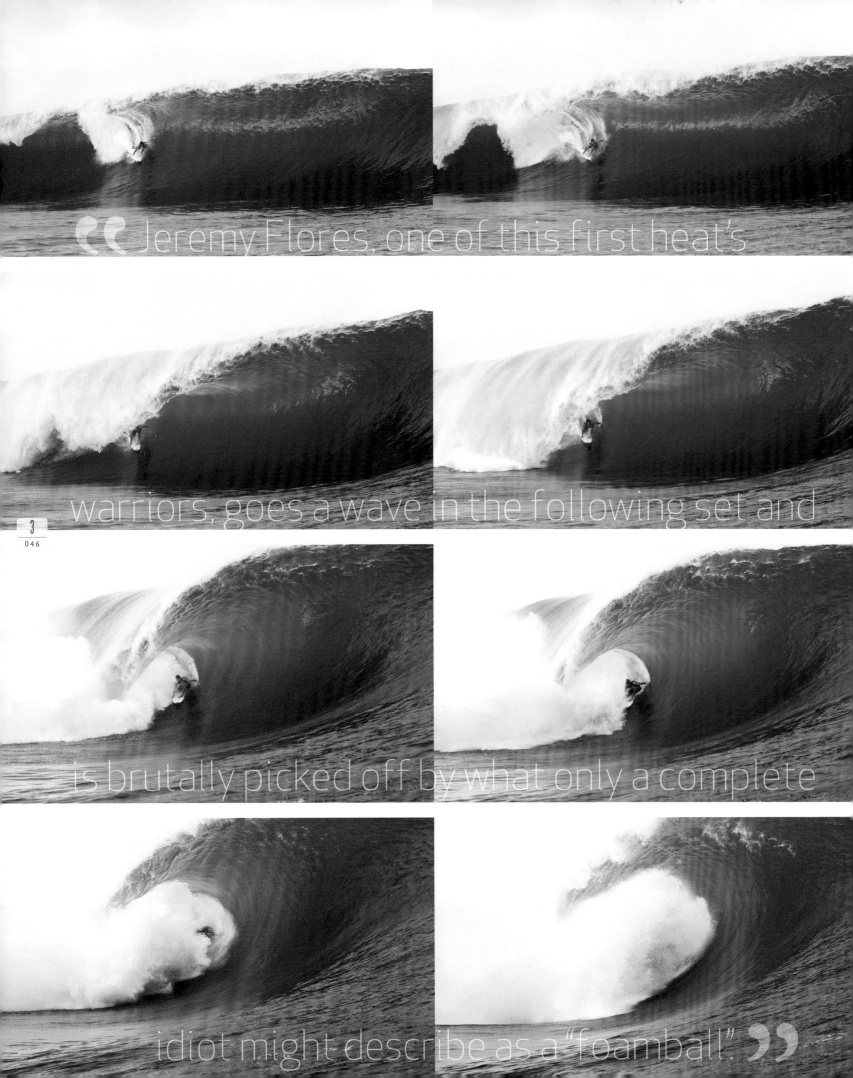

"Jeremy Flores, one of this first heat's warriors, goes a wave in the following set and is brutally picked off by what only a complete idiot might describe as a "foamball"."

JEREMY
FLORES

Davo and Kai Otton are watching the heat via webcast from Jonny Jenkins's house on the point, when Jeremy Flores, one of this opening heat's warriors, goes a wave in the following set and is brutally picked off by what only a complete idiot would describe as a "foamball".

"I'm honestly scared now," Davo says, wonderingly.

Then the truth flashes across his mind.

"They've been WAITING for TODAY to send us out to be flogged for everyone's entertainment, while they're all snuggled up at home watching the computer! My mates said they'll all be down at the Sands watching today, with a steak and a beer!"

He pauses, as the horror of this revelation sinks in. "I wanna be back at the Alley!"

By now they're both laughing, but then Heiarii Williams, the other warrior in this first heat, is sucked over the falls on a set wave and driven towards the reef.

The boys stop laughing at this point, and quietly begin discussing board choices. Suddenly it really matters. Because otherwise, as Kai says: "You feel like the wave is showing you around the lineup."

Jeremy Flores, the warrior, is not laughing either. After picking his way through and out of this first heat's terrible dicing, he gives voice to his anger. "I told the organisers afterward, you guys don't realise," he says. "It doesn't mean we're scared or anything – it's not safe here. It was messy with wind chops and big ones, man, I didn't want to go near it. I was psyched to go out there, but for safety it was a rad decision. It was super scary."

I think back to the afternoon of the day before: to Davo's instinct about this event, how it revolves somehow around *mana*, the Polynesian idea of life energy. And how if you want to connect with the mana, you have to throw yourself at it.

After surfing, he dives in the river, soaking in the fresh mountain rainwater, then drags me along on a crazed Bear Grylls style climb up the ridges behind the town, clinging idiotically to vines and bits of fern frond. Covered in shit and exhausted, we stand on the ridge peak and gaze down to the reef, where tiny barrels peel and spit, and tiny people try to ride 'em.

ALEJO
MUNIZ

3
048

I squint out to the south-western horizon, hundreds of nautical miles away, flat and calm and expressionless. Andy's gift is out there, somewhere, heading this way. You can't see it. But it's coming.

Now… it's here. Or is it.

Another terrifying heat goes by, then half of the third. Then Ace Buchan lifts it out of the fear-murk with a single ride. A near-freefall to rail set into a six-second barrel. It's a raw situation handled with the utter aplomb of a contender. It makes Teahupo'o rideable.

"Me and Pritamo (Ahrendt, head judge) hugged when we saw that wave," says O'Callaghan. "'Cause we knew it was going to come good."

It does, it so does. The wind swings flat trade offshore, the sky clears from its morning gloom, and the swell pulse settles, driving from deep on the reef at a challenging south-westerly angle, asking its hard and thrilling question with every set.

The Teahupo'o acid test can do strange things to the shape of a surfer's performance: give it new shape and structure, warp it into something odd and uncomfortable, or just burn it away entirely, like an errant leaf in a firestorm.

In Kai Otton's case, it outlines and magnifies his strengths and you can see his surfing clearer than ever. Kai walks into round four with a perfect 10 score under his belt and a quarterfinal beckoning. He is just ahead of Raoni Monteiro, who seizes his own 10 with a passionate furious line through the heart of one of the waves of the day.

Up in the judging tower, Pritamo warns his panel: Keep your heads. Be critical. Don't get involved in what the surfers are thinking or doing. Sit back, watch, compare waves with waves. But how do you do that, stay reasonable and rational on an eight to ten-foot day at this place, when people are jumping off cliffs every heat?

Parko will rue a decision or two from today, even though he tries to make light of it afterward: "The (world title) race hasn't even started yet – guys are just looking for a couple of keepers," he reckons. This isn't one of his keepers. Nor is it one of Adriano de Souza's, or Taj Burrow's.

It's one of Kerrzy's. Josh is one of the exciting surprises of the day, a former kid rebel who underneath it is sturdy as your grand-dad and is responding to Teahupo'o like a champ. He revenges himself lightly upon Julian Wilson after being clipped by Jules in their round one heat several days before, and is clearly in a mood to worry anyone he faces from here on in.

Maybe it'll be one of Owen Wright's. Owen, 21, mega-star in waiting, has been off line and out of rhythm in three of the four big events of 2011 so far, and scorched by a bad judging call in the fourth. He loses his first-round heat here… and something changes. A new, forceful, accurate intention behind his wave choice, line and length.

As the swell begins to back down, Jeremy Flores comes back from his fearful morning to record a superb win over Cory Lopez in one of the day's last heats. Kelly Slater, 39 and not feeling his age, watches Jeremy, then jumps in to ride some waves before dark.

It feels as if a better day can't be had. Surely Andy's gift has come and gone? But that afternoon, back in the village, new faces begin to appear – the big-wave tow-in crews. People who represent the flipside of modern surfing's bleeding-edge skill levels. People who are pulled towards things other people carefully walk around. They've flown in overnight from Hawaii, Australia, Brazil, the US: Nathan Fletcher, Makuakai Rothman, Laurie Towner, Ryan Hipwood, Koby Abberton, Keala Kennelly, Maya Gabeira, Dylan Longbottom, Dean Bowen, Everaldo Pato, a dozen others.

The forecast has created a kind of vortex into which all these great surfers are being sucked, almost despite themselves – sucked towards a place that is suddenly the perfect centre of the surfing universe. Worlds are colliding. And in the background is the arbiter itself, Teahupo'o.

In the face of the super-extreme surf forecast, the local government has declared a Code Red in all French Polynesian waters. In other words, no watercraft can leave their moorings, and people sure as hell aren't supposed to surf.

The event, should the swell allow it, has an exemption. The tow-in crews don't. But in the end, none of it will make a difference. ∎

3
053

JOSH
KERR

JOSH
KERR

BRETT
SIMPSON

C'MOOON!

CJ
HOBGOOD

KIEREN
PERROW

CHRIS
DAVIDSON

ALEX
GRAY

3
0.5.8

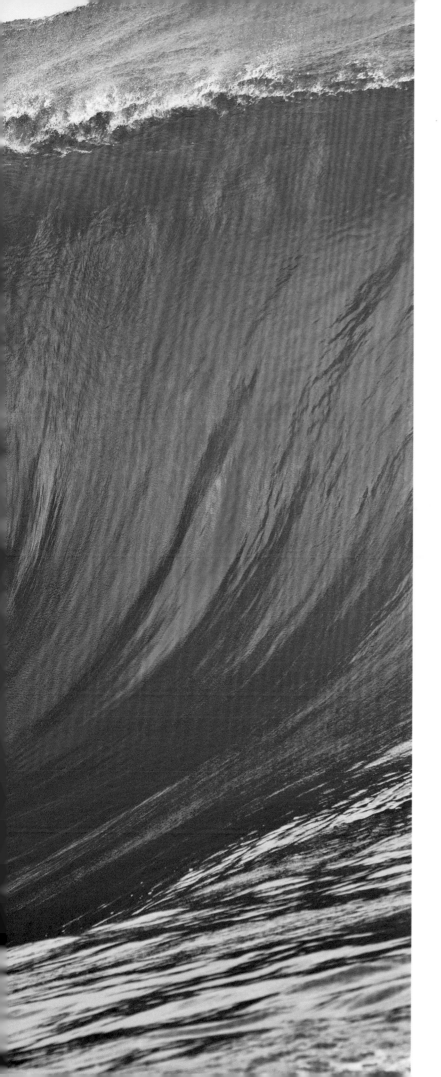

CODE RED

— 27 / 08 / 2011 —

WHERE NO
HUMAN
WAS MEANT
TO GO

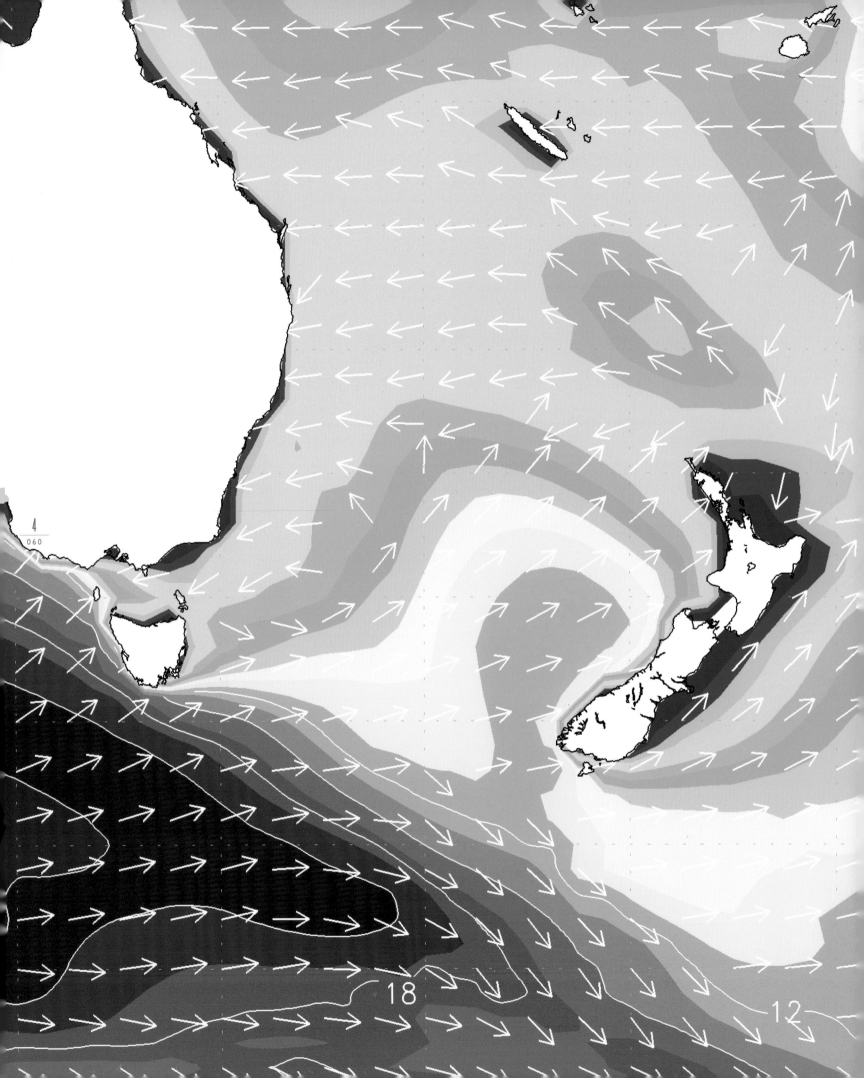

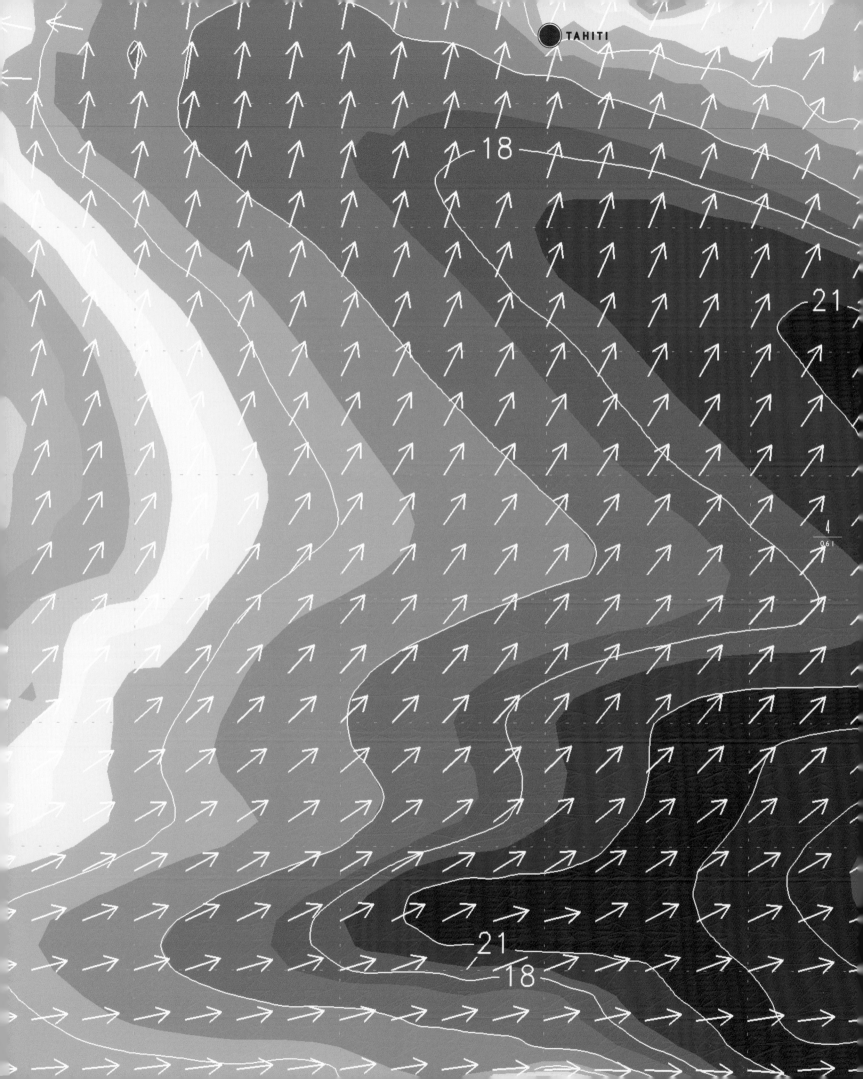

How often is it – in surfing or anything – you can truly say you've seen something you've never seen before ... Something you'll only ever see once?

Early in the morning of August 27 – or late the night before, depending on how you look at 2.00am – **the reef begins to boom.** Almost imperceptible, ground-shaking impacts.

At the crack we get up, have coffee and walk down to check it.

Immediately you can see it's BIG. Seawater has broken the berm protecting the lawns along the rim of the bay inside the pass; rocks and weed and bits of junk are scattered in unusual places. The dogs you normally see on those lawns are gone.

Kerrzy is on the roof of his house with a crew, sees Davo, and starts trying to prank him. "8.30 start!" he yells. "I'm serious!" He can't carry it off for even a second. We go up on to the roof to watch. The lagoon is draining off water like spilt beer off a kitchen table. A darkness is in the water, of old silts being stirred from somewhere deep.

I see a ski streaking across the lineup, surfer staying on the rope, and a ten-foot wave sliding under them both, the lip-line falling and the wave spitting hard into the channel.

Then behind it. Holy Shit. Twenty-foot-square slabs, twenty-five feet, thirty feet, one after another, hitting the reef and almost doubling in size. The whitewater explosion on the reef is almost twice the height of the lagoon tower. If human beings are on those waves, none of them make it to the channel.

You can hear people squealing down at the point several hundred metres away. The rush of water from the set has encircled the medical hut and is pulling the tip of the point apart. "Look at it!" says Kaimana Alexander, peering. "That thing's gonna be gone today."

Skis now come in over the reef, searching the lagoon for someone or something. The object of the search is Victor, a Brazilian surfer who has dislocated his left knee, blowing out all the ligaments. It turns out he'd let go on the small front-runner wave and been caught inside on the reef. The docs aren't supposed to get involved, but Mary, a paramedic with the event, runs over to check on him, and Woody from security alerts the ambulance at the marina three kilometres away. Victor is carted off behind his buddy's ski.

Now a ski seems to be adrift well out in the lagoon, just inside the reef line. Two other skis come over to it, gathering like animals around a fallen fellow. They're doing something, but what?

The skis come slowly into the point and off the back of one slides Raimana van Bastolaer, and he falls backward into the water and lies there looking up at the sky.

"Everyone ate shit," says Strider Wasilewski, who is on one of the skis. "Everyone."

Raimana struggles to his feet and very slowly makes his way up on to more or less dry land, where Luke Egan carefully helps him peel off his wetsuit. He has a deep grazed bruise all the way down his right side, from shoulder to knee. "I was in it," he says, meaning the wave, "and then it just swung around and threw me. I hit HARD, man."

"You were saved by your wetsuit," says Luke.

"And my PFD," says Raimana. The reef has torn him up through a life vest and a wettie.

Strider describes trying to drive his ski inside the foam line on the way to crossing the reef. "It just fell through a hole in the (water) surface," he says. "I was driving the ski completely underwater." He is shaking his head very slightly.

Makua Rothman comes in and around on a ski, his whole body posture alert and sharp. Keala Kennelly is up on the drowned lawn fringe with a knee brace and a tow-board. Everything about the scene clicks somewhere in the back of my mind, although I know I haven't quite seen its like. It feels almost fictional – as if there are people gathered here today not to surf, but to slay dragons.

We wait for the tide to fill a bit, then leap with boards into the channel inside the lagoon and head out to have a look. Swiftly the overflow sucks us out wide into the bay and we have to work through a lot of sucky water to break clear and finally be paddling well wide of the reef up to the wave itself.

By this time a dozen boats and several jetskis are trimming back and forth in the slot of deep water off to the side of the bowl, and a pack of surfers – Joel Parkinson, Pat Gudauskas, Ace Buchan, Julian Wilson, Rasta, Anthony Walsh, Owen Wright, Kerrzy – are spectating and playing chicken with the slot.

It feels almost fictional – as if there are people gathered here today not to surf, but to slay dragons.

They tell us about the carnage: Maya Gabeira going a smaller one, then being trapped inside on the reef between the end of the left and the nasty right on the other side of the slot for six set waves, unable to go out or back into the lagoon, her driver frozen by the circumstance and unable to act. Poto taking his own ski in and snatching her. Maya unable to speak and bleeding from an ear.

Dingo Morrison coming out of a good one a bit too high on the face, his board flipping beneath him with a foot still caught in a strap, maybe breaking an ankle.

"Danilo Costa went over backwards," says Kerrzy. "He was just in there," he says, pointing towards the reef. "But wasn't paying attention when a wave came. He went over and we never saw him again."

We're laughing and shaking our heads, when the water begins to drain seaward, and a wave with a face flat and black as basalt stands up across Teahupo'o reef. A ski is there, then it isn't, then a surfer is, running extremely fast in mid-face and angling down slightly. The black face is six or seven times his height and bending. For three or four seconds it looks as if the surfer will negotiate the bend. As he is doing this, people in the boats are screaming for their drivers to get clear, and people on their boards are scratching to make some ground. Then the wave hooks back into the reef at the last moment, 15 feet of lip pitch over and sideways, and the surfer's board buries itself nose-first in the resulting curve.

It's Bruce Irons.

Everyone is still screaming. We look down from the top of the next wave into the foamy madness inside and see him pop up, and give a thumbs up.

I instantly know why this scene has never quite connected with me before despite the years of incredible footage and photos of massive Chopes – because the intensity of it, the wildness, the distilled purity of the surfing experience, is impossible to convey. The words, the pictures, however dramatic, are just a pale shadow.

Several minutes pass and then a wave of unearthly dimensions, huge. The wave creates a space within itself that no human was ever meant to occupy. The surfer is Nathan Fletcher and he goes into that space anyway. The wave descends upon him and explodes with a force so terrible that it causes the water in the channel to shake.

Unbelievably Nathan is snatched clear by his driver and is OK. It's only water, or is it.

"You've been surfing for 40 years," says Parko, "ever seen that?" Not even close.

The wave is so big it causes everyone in the channel to forget everything for a little while. A kind of collective memory blackout.

Irons's next wave is like a smack in the face. It's almost as big as Nathan's and it blasts him equally fiercely. Maybe more so. His driver, Koby Abberton, races in after him, a look of concern on his face, but then when he gets to Bruce he starts laughing, and it's soon obvious why.

"It took my shorts," half yells Bruce. "Naked!" Koby is cracking up. He drives Bruce through all the boats, Bruce smacking his own bald arse, as if to say: "I don't care! Have a look if ya want!"

Something about Bruce's pantlessness suddenly humanises this outrageous circumstance. No longer is it completely surreal. The surfers in the channel begin to relax. Davo wonders if maybe he should try to grab a rope and have a go, but the moment passes.

Heaps of other guys get bombs and do wonders: Alex Gray, Walshy, Laurie Towner, Hippo, Freddy P, Sean Lopez, Keala, Rasta, Dean Bowen, numerous others of the pack of big-wave chargers who've been drawn here from across the world for this day's swell. Later, way later that arvo, I get back in and see they're webcasting the whole thing, and watch it for a while on screen to see if I could get even a little bit close to what had happened out there earlier. You couldn't. But I hadn't really expected to.

Instead I kept thinking of the place in the wave where none of them were supposed to go, and how they'd gone there anyway, the way Nate and Bruce had. Was there some price to pay for it, other than water up the nose and a reef cut or six? When we're all watching this, do we really know what we're seeing? Or is it just a show for the crowd?

> The wave creates a space within itself that no human was ever meant to occupy.

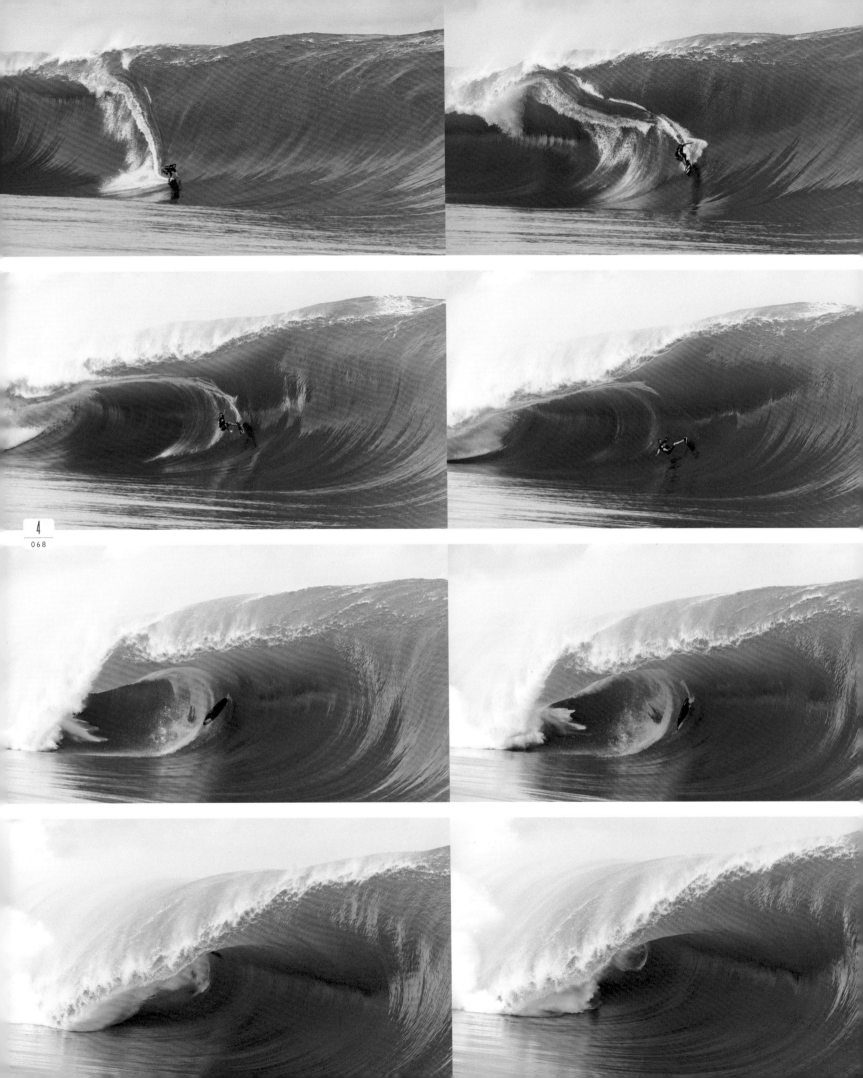

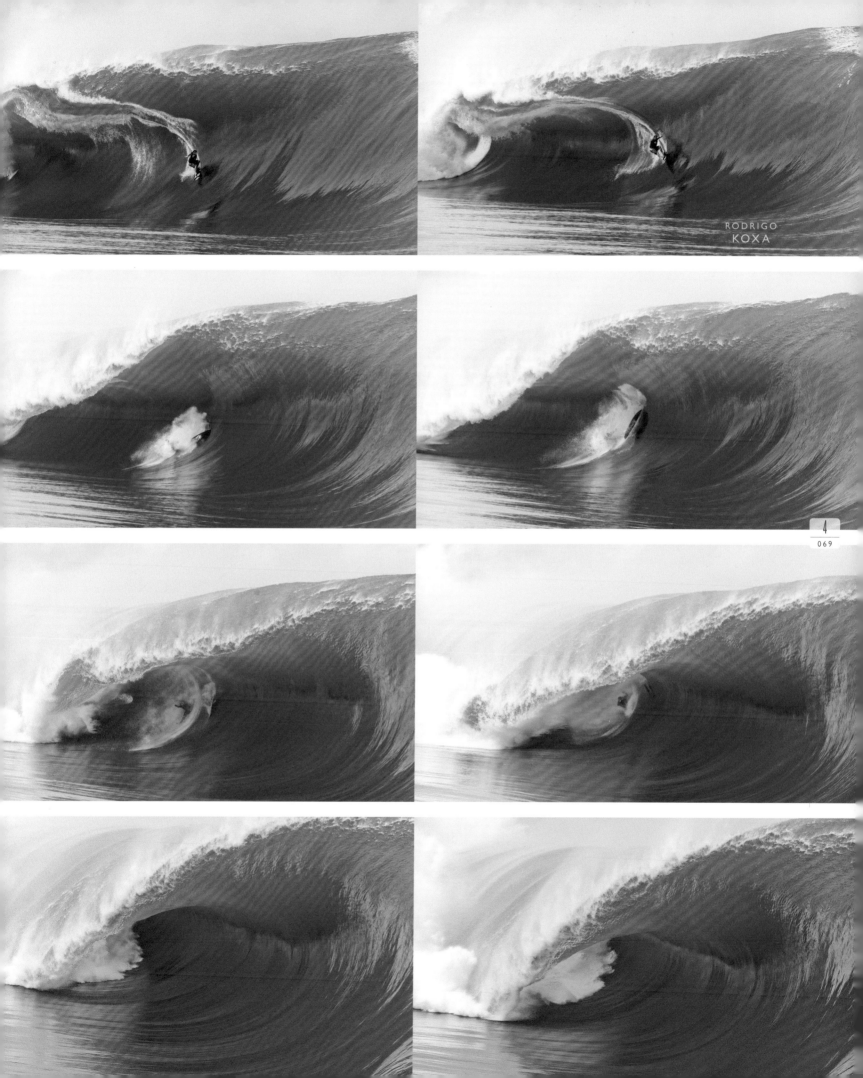

RODRIGO
KOXA

DEAN
BOWEN

BRUCE
IRONS

SEQUENCE
CONTINUES →

"The black face is six or seven
times his height ... people
in the boats are screaming
for their drivers to get clear,
and people on their boards
are scratching to make some
ground ... 15 feet of lip pitch
over and sideways."

WHO ARE THESE PEOPLE?

"Little Alex Gray!" Kerrzy screamed from the channel when the identity of this rider became clear. Little, big, or in between, the surfers who took on Teahupo'o on August 27 all showed us one thing: size matters, but not in the way you'd expect. Alex, fighting for a clear look at his fate, midday Saturday.

PHOTO: TED GRAMBEAU

060 ~ 061

RED EVERYWHERE

And so it hits. Countless surfers worldwide tracked Surfline's swellmaps with eager disbelief as bands of red morphed and marched to their target. Sure enough, as predicted, there it was.

IMAGE: SURFLINE

064 ~ 065

YOUR WAVE

There were empty ones pouring through the lineup, almost daring someone to have a crack at a paddle-in. Eventually someone did, only to be pitched off the end bowl before he could get to his feet. That wave was about four feet smaller than this one, which one assumes makes this one completely unrideable. Yours if you want it.

PHOTO: TED GRAMBEAU

068 ~ 069

TOO HIGH, TOO SOON

Rodrigo Koxa provides an object lesson in the horribly fine lines being walked at Teahupo'o that incredible day. He makes a small correction at the wave base designed to place him square to the line; instead the wave draws him fractionally too high … and he's gone. Thank God for the PFD.

PHOTOS: TIM MCKENNA

070 ~ 071

JUST HIGH ENOUGH

Dean Bowen put on two PFDs – one small, one large, to increase flotation and to reduce the chances of a loose neck line catching water in a wipeout and ripping the whole thing clean off. Thus equipped, he felt more or less ready to take on things that make his left reef down the coast look like a Goldie beachbreak on a bad day. Deano, driving out of the centre.

PHOTO: TIM MCKENNA

072 ~ 075

THE WAVE THAT FREAKED THE CHANNEL

Bruce Irons on his first mammoth. The situation was too much for numerous spectators, who panicked and screamed at their boat drivers to get clear at all costs. Bruce didn't have that option. Moments after the last shot of this sequence, he nosedived into the end bowl curve… only to surface 20 seconds later, giving his freaked-out mates in the channel a big thumbs up.

PHOTO: TIM MCKENNA

076 ~ 077

THE WAVE THAT GOT HIS SHORTS

Within 15 minutes, Teahupo'o had disrobed him, much to the amusement of Kerrzy (right) and everyone else, including ski driver Koby Abberton, who took Bruce on a little parade through the channel crowd, as if to say "What the hell! we're only human!" It broke the spell of a mid-morning session that until then had felt unearthly, hard to watch and impossible to imagine.

PHOTOS: THOUARD + GRAMBEAU

AT RIGHT

THE MARK OF DOOM

On normal days (see bottom pic) the big yellow channel anchor mark sits so far clear of the reef you could almost sit a cup of tea on it. On August 27 it became a kind of DMZ indicator; stay outside it and you'd probably be OK, sneak inside it and be ready for the fright of your life… or worse. What would you risk for a view?

PHOTOS: GRAMBEAU + DAWE

080 ~ 081

SOME PEANUT GALLERY

Part of the madness of the day was the fact that Teahupo'o lets you in so close to its banging trapdoor you can feel it slamming shut. In a boat you can almost begin to fool yourself that you're safe, and that 15-foot-thick lip within a camera-throw can't possibly get you. Until one swings wider than usual… and the throttles go forward real quick. Everaldo Pato, where the boats really don't want to go.

PHOTO: TED GRAMBEAU

" In a boat, you can almost begin to fool yourself that you're safe, and that 15-foot-thick lip within a camera-throw can't possibly get you. Until one swings wider than usual… and the throttles go forward real quick. "

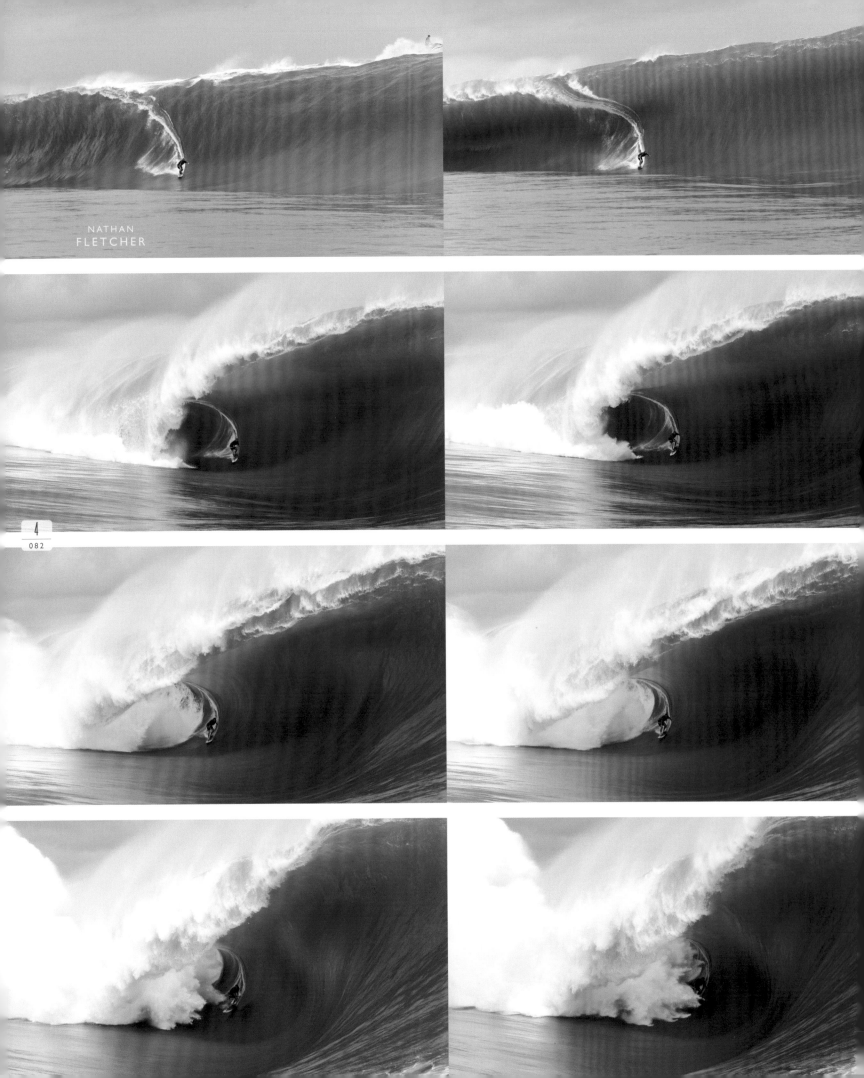

NATHAN
FLETCHER

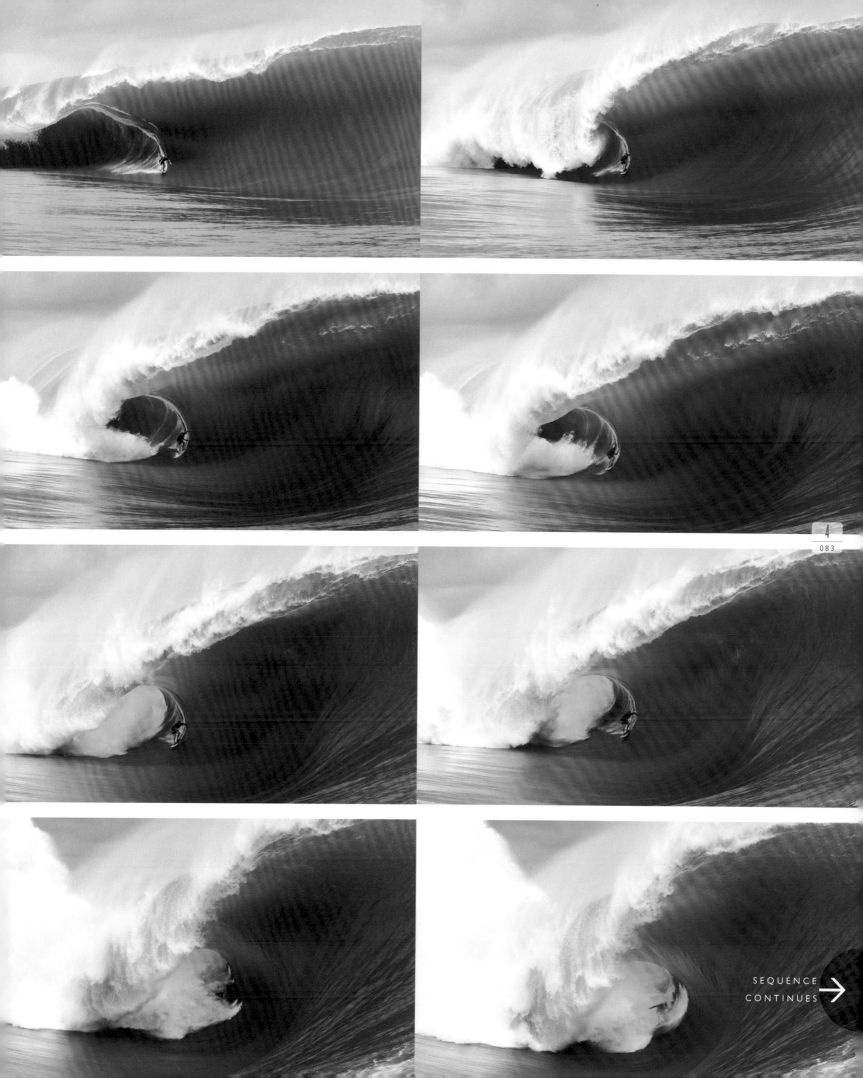

SEQUENCE CONTINUES →

> " The wave creates a space
> within itself that no human
> was ever meant to occupy.
> The surfer is Nathan Fletcher
> and he goes into that space
> anyway. "

SEQUENCE
CONTINUES →

LAURIE
TOWNER

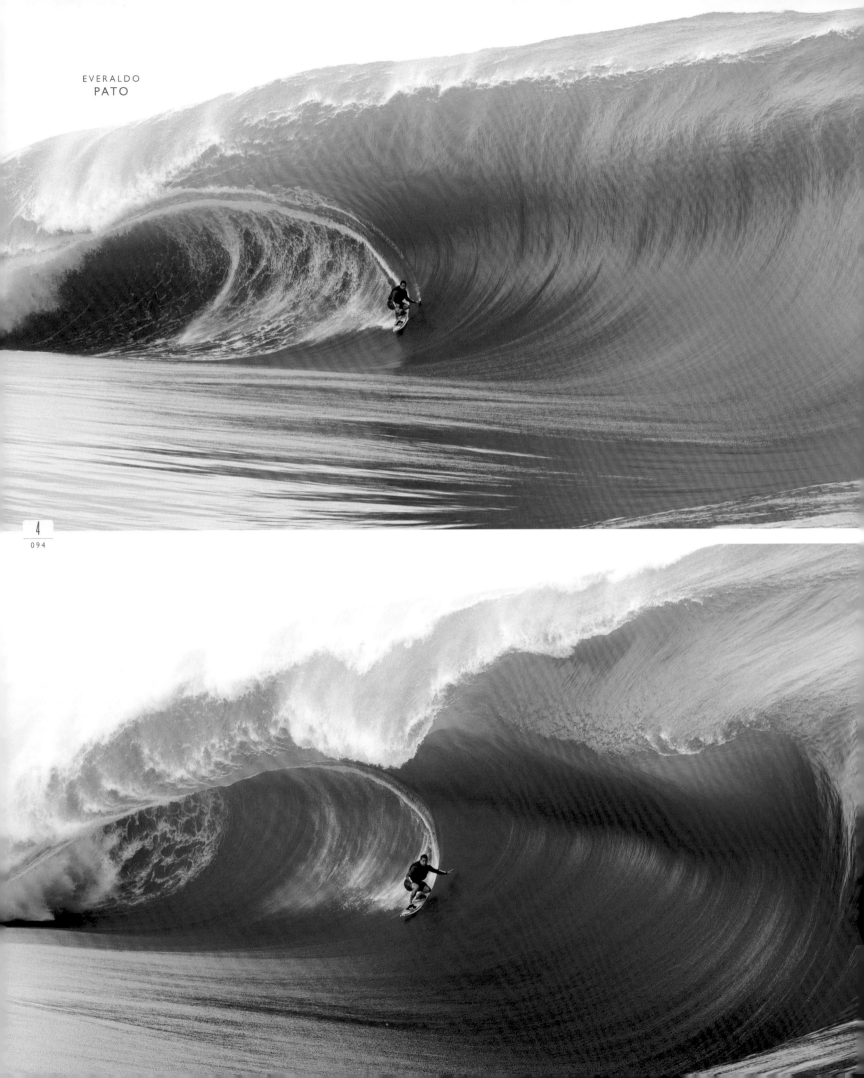

SEQUENCE
CONTINUES →

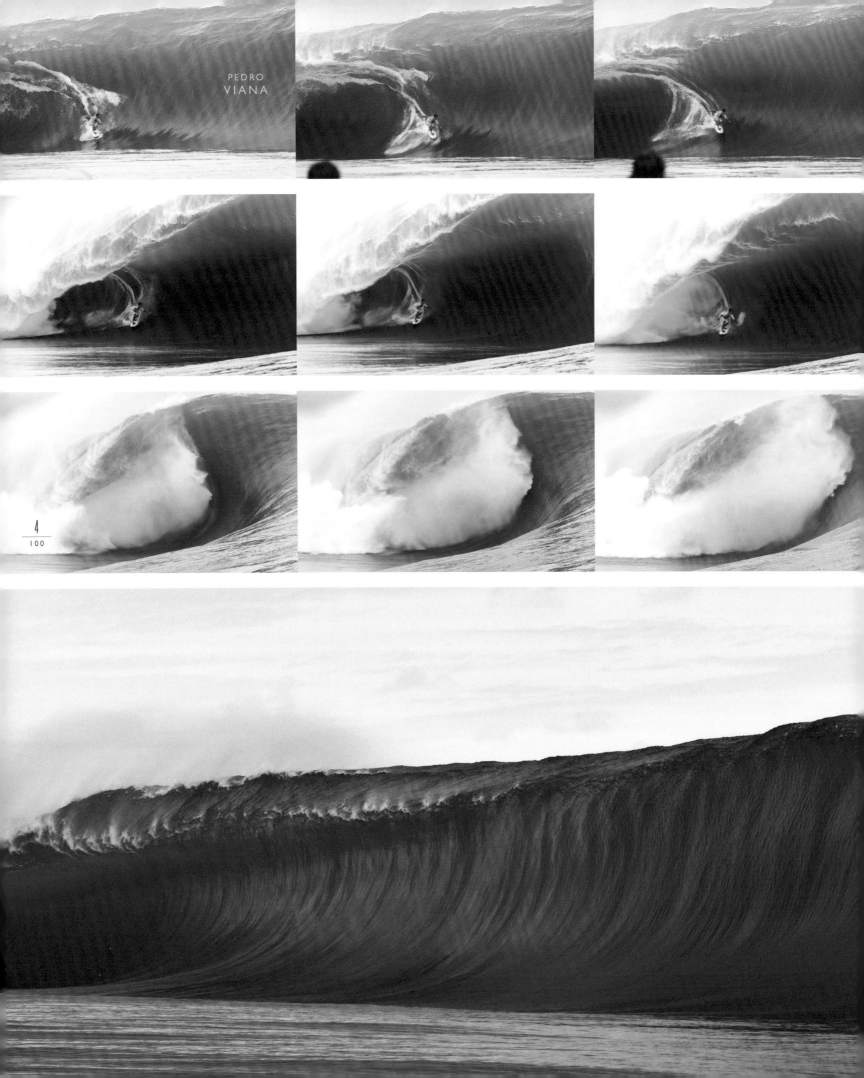

PEDRO
VIANA

4
___
100

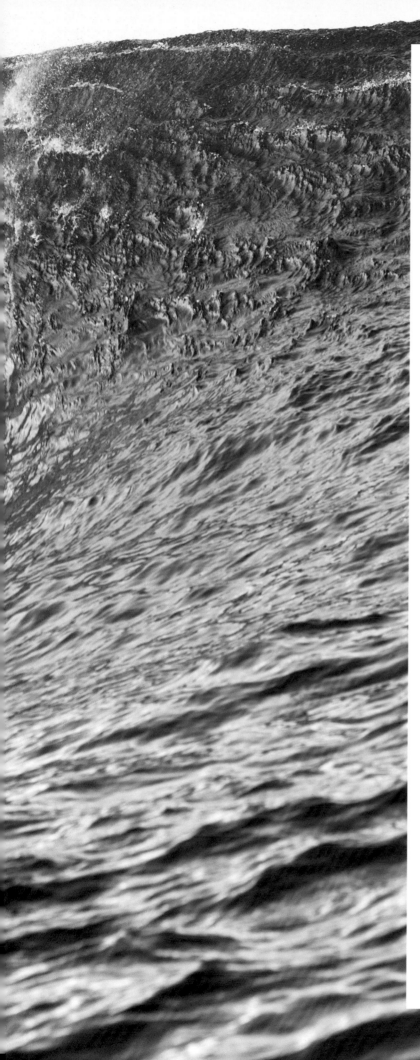

Next morning it is silk glass again and eight to ten feet on the sets, and the baton is handed back to the pro elite, who seize it and produce an overwhelmingly strong day of competitive surfing.

The day brings forth trends. Slater, easy and masterful in the conditions, advancing without ever stretching his skills. Kerrzy, winning his three-man fourth-round heat with two waves and without even wetting his hair. Brett Simpson, one of the tour's big pit rookies, discovering his inner Chopes Grommet and beating one of his heroes, Damien Hobgood. Owen, staying on message in ever more ominous and unflinching fashion, finishing with a superb relaxed 10.

It brings forth injuries. Funny ones, like Matt Wilkinson's bum scrape. Wilko talks like he is scared of Teahupo'o, but he's changing his career at this event; two perfect scores in three days, and more lime juice per square centimetre of body tissue than any other competitor. "My whole body's a scab," he laughs, showing where the razorblades have cut through his boardies. "Maybe I'll be better-looking after this contest is finished."

And nasty ones, like Jordy Smith's broken rib. Deep in a morning barrel, Jordy falls and is clipped by his surfboard's rail. In agony he's dragged clear, contorting on a jetski sled in the channel. Courage and desire get him back into the lineup for a re-surf, against old buddy Travis Logie; the weight of the pain drags him down. It'll be three events before he's ready again.

It brings forth a perfect heat, only the fourth one in history. Jeremy Flores, yesterday's near-sacrifice, produces an epic late, steep, drop-barrel combination, and the panel gives it a 10. Then he gets a better one. "It went all the way," he says later. "But I thought no way they're giving me another 10! Not ME!" They do, and Jeremy is floored. He comes in and walks up the beach to the huts, passing Joel Parkinson on the way; Parko, one of the three others to get a 20/20, grins and says: "Welcome to the club."

Worlds have collided here this year, and already the surfing universe is feeling the impact. Tens of millions of people worldwide are staring slack-jawed at their TVs and computer screens, wondering whether or not to believe what they've seen off this tiny piece of rural Tahitian coastline. But one more day is yet to play out – and nothing about it will be simple. ■

JOSH
KERR

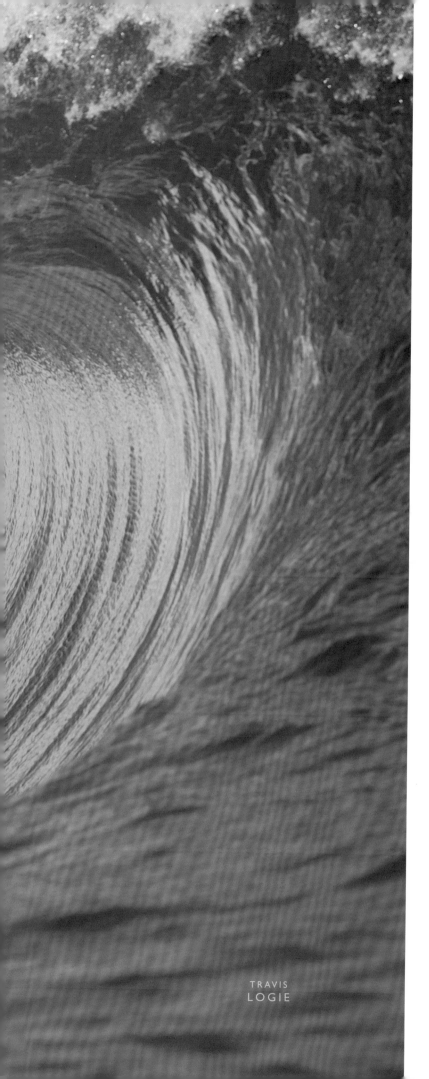

TRAVIS
LOGIE

AFTERGLOW

5
109

— 29/08/2011 —

WHERE BOTH
SWELL AND SCORES
ARE SETTLED
ON FINALS DAY

KELLY
SLATER

The truth is, this whole scene peaked two days ago, and everyone here knows it. Today, August 29, finals day, with its dewy dawn and splendid six foot plus creamy morning barrels, is the declension,

it's the bit in the movie where you sigh with relief, knowing everything's kinda back to normal **and nobody else is going to be killed by the zombies.**

Through the day I keep running into the hell-men of Saturday; to a hell-man, they're sated. Not tired exactly, just full of whatever mental food they must crave in order to be driven into zones like those that existed on that reef 48 hours ago.

There is Hippo, enjoying a mid-afternoon beer as he gazes out across the lagoon, and looking – if I may be blunt – as if he's just had a huge amount of sex. "Just been… cruising," he says, surrounded by the radiance of his own smile. Up the beach walks Everaldo Pato, the Brazilian charger who got the wave of his life only to have it mis-ID'ed on a big US website. "Can you ask for it to be corrected?" he says, but he just doesn't sound like it matters.

Strider Wasilewski is puttering around on the same ski from August 27 – the one he'd driven underwater, after that day's first major set blew the lineup apart. "Feeling… great," he says, smiling exactly the same sort of smile as Hippo's.

Dean Bowen's trying not to think about the flight home. Free-surfing after yesterday's competition had finished, Deano did what Dusty tried to do, and landed on his arse and lower back, hard. Now he's covered in surgical gauze and tape and sitting in the local snack bar, ordering pizza and wincing slightly with every move.

But there is still a contest out there to win; still eight surfers with their claws in the wave face, in the hunt for the win that everyone now knows will define 2011.

Kelly Slater has been at play here so far, loosening up, as he often does in early rounds. Look-back barrel exits, cheeky wave selection, experimenting with the lineup and its many subtle variations. Today he drops all that and engages fully with the samurai art of competition. One wave in his quarterfinal with Wilko makes it clear. While Matt sits and waits for a bomb, Kelly paddles away from him, deep on to the reef, where a super-steep, wicked, six-foot A-frame stands up to say hello. Slater drops in late and a little behind and executes one turn, deadly precise and half-squared off the base. The resulting line, through and beneath an already pitching, pinching lip, is unflinching as Teahupo'o's own.

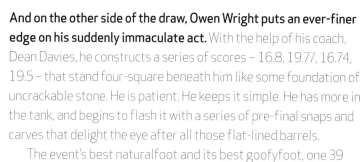

OWEN
WRIGHT

And on the other side of the draw, Owen Wright puts an ever-finer edge on his suddenly immaculate act. With the help of his coach, Dean Davies, he constructs a series of scores – 16.8, 19.77, 16.74, 19.5 – that stand four-square beneath him like some foundation of uncrackable stone. He is patient. He keeps it simple. He has more in the tank, and begins to flash it with a series of pre-final snaps and carves that delight the eye after all those flat-lined barrels.

The event's best naturalfoot and its best goofyfoot, one 39 years old and the other 21, fall into the final together as if it couldn't have happened any other way.

But first: in honour of his champion brother, Bruce Irons is scheduled to surf. He invites eight or 10 friends into the water with him. Bruce's first move is a huge throwaway air off the lip of the bowl section. In a declining swell, guards are down, and the relaxed vibe of the afterglow floods across the lineup.

Keala Kennelly's guard is down. Parko hoots her into a wicked, deep, drivey five-footer. Keala, who'd towed into a 15-footer on Saturday, ate it, and went straight back out and got another one, rides this wave all the way in towards the place where Dusty and Dean met the razorblades… and is picked off. The right side of her head slams directly on to coral-plated reef and opens a star-shaped cut from above her eye all the way to the jawline and across the cheekbone. A laceration so deep that Dr Fischer, back at the medical hut, can see her eye muscles working. After over 100 incidents in recent years, it's the worst injury he's ever treated.

The water patrol is so quick to grab Keala and get her to land that almost nobody realises what has happened.

As the finalists cruise into position, a light wind hesitates on the brink of swinging onshore, then changes its mind. Conditions are holding near to perfect… but the set-wave rhythm has slowed.

Owen, six feet three inches of completely focused human, goes to priority and waits for the waves he wants, like he has for the past four heats. But Kelly's been watching and is alert to the slight decline in swell energy. He decides to play it the other way; roams the lineup, picking waves off while Owen waits. He's scratching towards his third when the panel scores his first a 9.5 out of 10.

Owen holds his nerve. "You can't stop Kelly doing his thing," he says later. "I was out there to choose my waves and he was out there to choose his." He uses his as wisely as he can, but the bombs of the morning aren't there. The last two minutes pass with the surfers locked together, Owen trailing but holding his wave-choice card, Kelly leading and hoping Teahupo'o doesn't pitch some last-moment scene stealer into the mix … which she doesn't.

Kelly has shaken off an awkward misfire at the last major event to win this one in a way perhaps only he could have managed. "I never felt like I was the standout guy, I was getting my waves, winning my heats," he says. "Then I felt as I got into the semis and quarters, then I could throw everything at it."

108 ~ 109
ABOVE THE CALL

Travis Logie surfed one of the quietly great events of the year in making it to third place. Injured under the radar of his earlier heat against compatriot Jordy Smith, he battled a weakened shoulder, rankings pressure, and many expectations in these amazing silk-lined barrels, beaten only by the most in-form surfer of the contest. Trav, taking out Brett Simpson before he got to Owen, finals day.

PHOTO: HILTON DAWE

110 ~ 111
WITNESSING

Surely, the best place to be in the world on a fine August morning. Channel pundits soaking up sun and salt water, finals day

PHOTO: HILTON DAWE

112 ~ 113
TIME TO SHINE

Kelly Slater sensibly passed on surfing Big Saturday. His point of view: if you're not 100% ready for the biggest wave of the day, you're better off watching. On August 29 he was 100% ready to win any and every heat he had to, with some of the cleanest no-bullshit surfing you'll ever see. KS, deadly casual backside backdoor line, quarterfinals.

PHOTO: TIM MCKENNA

114 ~ 115
RISING TO THE TOP

Owen was carrying a new scar from a recent surf trip's reef headbutt. You could have been excused for wondering if it concealed a surgical implant designed to make him into the Perfect Competitor. Heat after heat, he sat and waited for the best ones, took off deep, and flawlessly judged the lines he needed to take. O saying Kelly here I come, semifinals.

PHOTOS: TED GRAMBEAU

AT RIGHT
WINNERS ARE GRINNERS

In the end it came down to experience, superior tactics, and a lull in the last two minutes. Increasingly this is how Slater wins – like a great distance runner, controlling the pace, never doing more than he needs, and keeping the best for last, so you almost don't see it coming. Almost. KS with mine host Raimana, celebrating another fizzy moment in a near-impossible career.

PHOTO: HILTON DAWE

118 ~ 119
ANDY'S REAL GIFT

It wasn't the swell; it was the willingness and ability to charge it on its own terms. AI was the master of the situation at this most heart-stopping of surf spots; this wave, ridden during the last major year (2002) in the contest's history, the one when he laid first claim to a world crown, will never be forgotten. The AI Forever Award for most committed surfer of the contest should help too. Winner Jeremy Flores with brother Bruce.

PHOTO: TOM SERVAIS

120 ~ 121
AFTER THE GOLDRUSH

Most of the competitors are gone that night. They have appointments to keep, new quivers to pick up, a precious couple of nights at home before the circus pitches tent in somewhere perhaps not as completely amazing as this. But if your plane is delayed a day, or there's no need to rush off, it's not a complete tragedy. Lucky fellow, pitted in a lonely lineup.

PHOTO: TIM MCKENNA

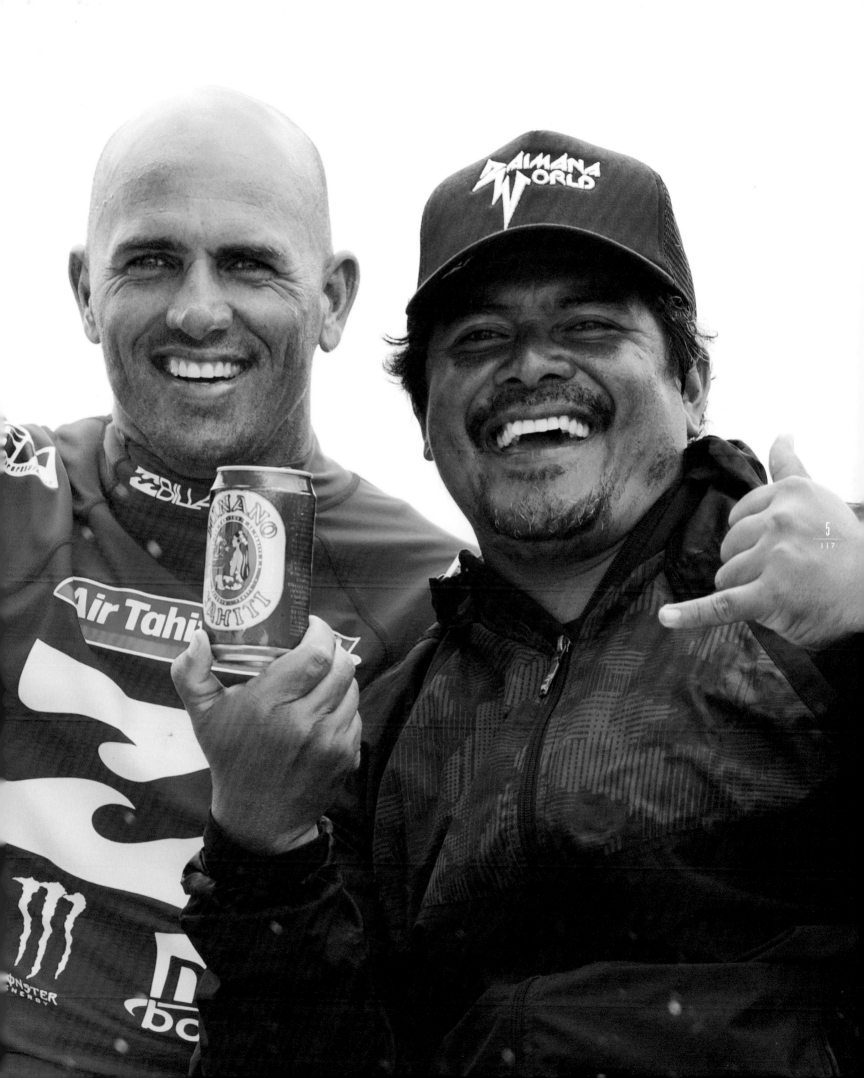

delayed, or there's no need to rush off, it's not a complete tragedy. **"**

So the movie comes to an end; the credits roll, the pro surfing world stands up, stretches and heads slowly for the exits…

Except it's not a movie, is it. It all really happened. The whole scene has been reset, realigned. In the months to come, the World Tour will take off into the stratosphere under pressure from the new competitive energies unleashed here at Teahupo'o. Owen and Kelly will fight out two more finals in a row, making three back-to-back, the first time such a thing has ever happened. Nathan's wave and Bruce's wave will be scorched on to the covers of almost every surf magazine on earth.

The past 10 days will have altered – subtly maybe, but clearly altered – **everything we thought we knew about what can be done by humans on waves.**

But it hasn't altered Teahupo'o. It's still a 10,000-year-old reef pass in the middle of the Pacific Ocean and **it will still do what it will do, whether we're there to ride it or not.**

We thought we knew Teahupo'o. **We still don't.** But we're closer.

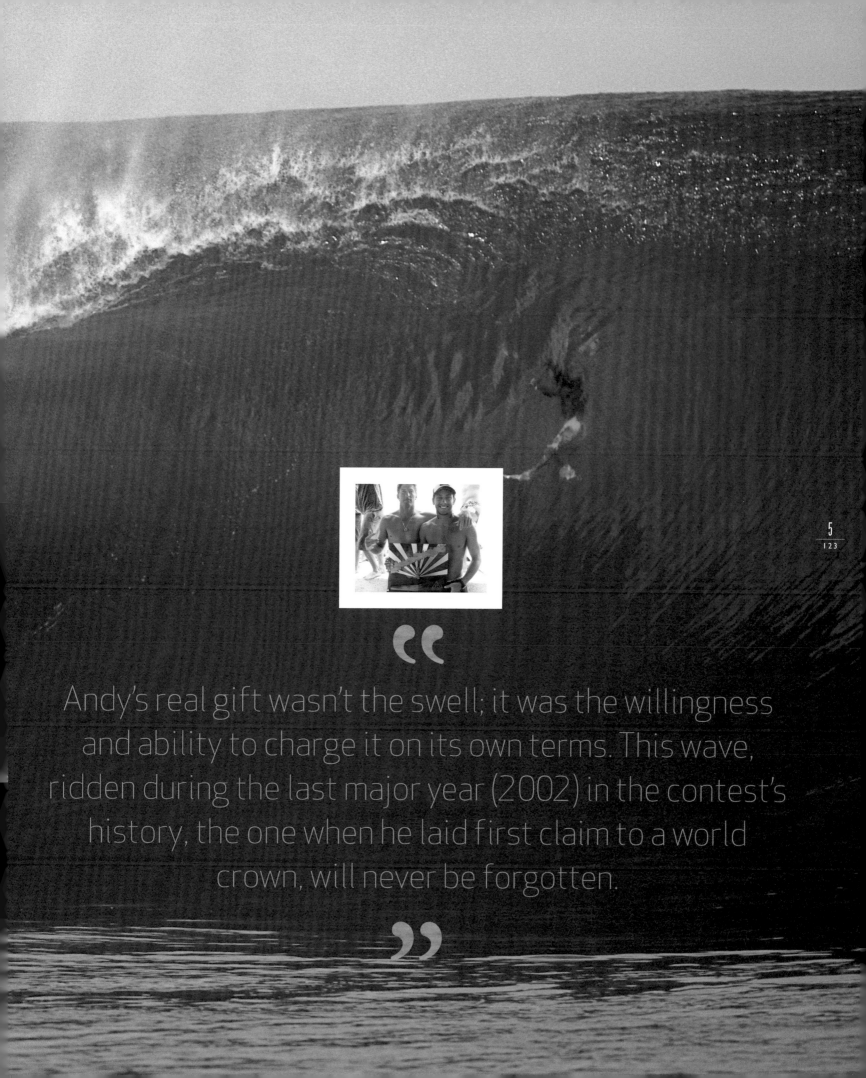

"

Andy's real gift wasn't the swell; it was the willingness and ability to charge it on its own terms. This wave, ridden during the last major year (2002) in the contest's history, the one when he laid first claim to a world crown, will never be forgotten.

"

IN
THEIR

OWN WORDS

BEHIND THE SCENES,
REFLECTIONS,
STORIES &
ACKNOWLEDGEMENTS

NEVER-ENDING STORY

As event director **Mick Talbot** explains, putting on this gig takes some doing,

The whole process starts the moment you unpack the two shipping containers from the previous year's comp. As soon as you pull gear out of the container you're starting to sort it for next year.

Two months before the comp, the containers are all packed up and good to go. They get shipped over and generally arrive in Tahiti a fortnight before the event. We get the guys set up in a house and Margo (freesurfing legend and our logistics fella) sorts out what goes where, what's gotta go to the webcast HQ, what's gotta go to the surfers' area, the tower, etc.

Everything that heads across in the containers is itemised on a massive list (featured on the closing pages of this book) and has to be accounted for, from a $2 roll of masking tape to a $20,000 jetski. Everything that goes in has to come back out: the Tahitian Government are pretty picky about that.

Apart from two jetskis and a few tinnies, there isn't a lot we leave over there from year-to-year.

The Tahitian Surfing Federation are fantastic, they manage the on-ground logistics with the key crew. Chris O'Callaghan is an expat Aussie who's been over there for a couple of decades, and he manages the relationships between Billabong and the local crew who are involved.

The tower out on the reef is a big job. You're building a complex structure in the middle of nowhere at the end of the road in the middle of the reef. Construction starts eight weeks ahead of the event. It really takes two weeks to build, but you're limited to working on days when the swell's less than a couple of feet – there can't be any water movement in the lagoon.

There are pylons in the reef that were put in years ago, carefully designed with the reef's shape and minimal impact in mind. Already

coral's growing around the pylons and they're home to all sorts of fish.

The wood comes out on a barge with a team of eight guys and they literally start building off the side of the boat. They link up with the pylons and build up from there. Ladder, first floor, second floor, third floor, roof. Chris and the local guys do a hell of a job. It's an impressive structure. The tower design gets refined and tweaked every year. This year's model passed the test nicely on the big day.

We've got such a good relationship with the crew over there, the

PIC: TALBOT

THE TOWER DESIGN GETS REFINED AND TWEAKED EVERY YEAR. THIS YEAR'S MODEL PASSED THE TEST NICELY ON THE BIG DAY.

freight crew and the local surfing fraternity. You have to be super methodical. We're as organised as you can be. But still, you're in Tahiti, and some things run on island time.

There's so many people and things to co-ordinate: There's a 28-person webcast team, eight cameras running, there's media crew from 15 different countries, there's six doctors, including two chiros, we send over an electrician, a sound engineer, a signwriter, a jetski mechanic and the list goes on. We're sending 100-plus people there so we're co-ordinating lots of travel and transfers, not to mention the 30-plus families to host 'em all.

We've got a relationship with Universal Music so we had The Living End and Colbie Callait come over – they kind of got added at the last moment – just when you think you're maxed out something new'll get thrown in over the top. But that's the beauty of Tahiti, you're working with such a cool group of people who'll do what needs to be done to make it happen, and there's no place for excuses 'cos there's nowhere else you can go.

The catering's all done locally. There's one full-time restaurant in Teahupo'o, but they set up a dozen restaurants there for a month – the school holidays and the comp period – then take 'em down two days after the event when everybody's gone.

We've cut our time over there from two months to five and a half weeks. We've refined our act to reduce the impact on the local area.

There's always challenges from year-to-year. Some things get lost in translation between teams or nationalities: like the Tahitian water patrol are 13 amazing watermen who you'll absolutely trust

EVERY YEAR WE PACK THE CONTAINER WITH MERCH AND SAY 'SURELY THERE'S ENOUGH THIS TIME' ...

PIC: TALBOT

your life to, but working with English-speaking doctors, there are sometimes communication issues and spur of the moment decisions need to be made in the heat of action that may not go according to the original plan. Just little communication things like that. Hardly surprising when you've got 40 radios on the go.

It's funny, it's such a well-oiled machine now that we never trip over the big stuff, but it's the little things that get ya on event days: Not having enough merchandise for everyone: there's always a kid down the road misses out on a cap. Every year we pack the container with merch and say "SURELY there's enough this time" … and every year it seems some little fella down the road misses out. Hopefully it's not the same kiddie each time though. That'd be too sad.

So we get the world's best surfers out on the world's most amazing wave, in the most amazing location, with the most amazing webcast ever, and you know where we fall short? Getting snacks out to the water patrol and chocolate out to the cameramen. Like I said, it's the little things.

The mega swell made things interesting. Steve Roberston's done the event for 12-odd years, ever since the Gotcha days, and he said he'd never seen anything like what he saw on the swell charts. We had legal counsel fly over when it became clear the swell was going to be mega, and we were in constant discussions with the Tahitian Surfing Federation and the Tahitian Government. We knew things were going to get crazy so we knew we had to do absolutely the right thing as far as safety and responsibility went. In the end the Government took some decisions out of our hands by issuing the Code Red: it was too big to paddle out or clearly run the event, so people did it at their own risk.

Even the day after Code Red it was so heavy there was still serious consideration for the health and safety of the crew. But we knew we had a good team and were so well drilled we were confident and good to go, we had it covered.

It was the most effort we'd ever had to invest in terms of so much happening in one event. The five and a half weeks I was there, there was so much going on.

Once the last ski is in from the final and once the last container door's shut you can kind of relax. But in reality it never ends. You get back to Australia and it loops around and you start again.

This year made all the four-foot years feel worthwhile. They were all great events, but in a way they were years of refining the management and running of the thing. You get a year like this and it's like "OK, this is why we do it".

Ironically, you don't get to see too much of the event on the water over there. You might catch a heat here or there, but you're running around doing so much it's not 'til the end of the day where you see a clip and you'll say "We got some pretty good waves". But that was cool, no matter where you were or what you were doing this year, the buzz was amazing. ∎

HUMAN DING REPAIR

Head of medical staff **Dr Paul Fischer** on what you need to be ready for.

I've been coming to the Teahupo'o event for four years. This is my 11th World Title tour event and this is definitely from my perspective the most scary, and with the most potential for serious injury and even death. With the big swell coming, we really needed to be on our toes to prepare for every eventuality.

Last year we had roughly 80 consultations. We saw a lot of patients. Most of them were non-competitors: webcasters, photographers, event support staff, hitting the reef predominantly. Tiger lacerations basically, that's what we saw. One was really bad, head, armpit, down to the pelvis, he hit the reef on his right side and was severely lacerated. Also, we saw an eight-year-old boy who'd been hit in the head by a golf club. That was a bit out of the box. Luckily, a year down the track, the kid is OK.

This year before the contest event started we had a pretty severe toe laceration, with a tendon exposed that we could see. Since then there's been some bad ones, Dusty's knee and Jordy's broken rib and cartilage. Keala Kennelly's injury was definitely the worst I've ever seen at a surfing event.

We prepare the plans and equipment for about six weeks before coming here. Then once we're here we do sorties, or dummy runs, getting a trauma from the break to the point. We have meetings and practices with the water patrol, having a patient brought in with different scenarios, such as unconscious, not breathing, head injury, and then meet them with oxygen and a spinal board and bring them into our resuscitation room here. Then we activate the local ambulance. Teahupo'o is tricky because you're cut off from pickup by the river, and we were going to have to carry people over the bridge by foot. This year's great because we've got a 4WD ambulance, so now they can drive across the creek and come around and pick them up right here. Then we'll take them to Papeete.

The other thing we've had to think about this year is the possibility of a boat going over the falls on to the reef. A mass-casualty situation. We've duplicated our resuscitation area and we've also discussed a disaster management plan with the local medical facility, which is pretty limited. If that sort of situation arose, from the medical point of view, we would go into our disaster management protocols, which is essentially triaging all the people, working out their airway and breathing and circulation, then also activating the local medical people. We have a local doctor on the event too and local paramedics, and we'd bring them in there.

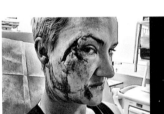

PIC: KK

KEALA KENNELLY'S INJURY WAS DEFINITELY THE WORST I'VE EVER SEEN AT A SURFING EVENT.

And then there's the unthinkable event of the tower collapsing. We've thought about that. It's up to the event organisers to make sure it's safe and can stand up to anything. The other concern that we have in a massive swell is the potential of the whole point being flooded, so we have to have a plan to relocate all our equipment. In 1998 the locals said the water came right up here to the hut.

As far as the psychology of it goes, I head a trauma unit at an Australian hospital so I'm used to seeing things, it would take a bit to shock me. But I know it's not like that for everyone and it's certainly not like that for the surfers. They want to know that arrangements have been made for their safety, but beyond that, in my experience, they sorta want to avoid us. Because when we start talking about what we've got and what we're ready for, they get nervous. They get scared when I talk about head injuries, or open leg wounds, and that sort of thing. So they just try not to talk about it. They want to talk about other things. ∎

HEART + HEAD

Accurate judging requires emotion kept at bay. Not always easy writes Head Judge **Pritamo Ahrendt**.

I look forward to being head judge at this one, for sure. It's an incredible wave to watch and it's a really easy wave to analyse in a way, because it's just about barrels. You don't have to watch a wave that's really long and compare 10 different manoeuvres with whatever's gone before. But in another sense it's super hard because you've got to be really critical in your judgements. People are getting really good barrels and you have to be harsh and willing to say it's just a six or a five, because there are absolutely incredible ones coming through, and you have to leave room in the scale. You have to leave room for the 10. You can't just get excited and throw high scores.

It's an interesting wave because although they're all barrels, there's different types of waves within that. So we've got to decide which are more critical and harder to ride. There's some barrels that may be slightly longer but have a thinner lip line and easy to thread, as opposed to the full free-fall drop into a barrel that may be shorter but way more heavy and intense. You have to consider which is harder to do out there, and I think commitment and degree of difficulty are the points in the criteria that we look to there.

I think the takeoff here is so much more important than any other spot on tour except maybe Pipeline, because it takes so much commitment to get in under the lip on the waves that are barrelling right on takeoff, and to be able to slide straight off the takeoff and be into the barrel and pumping through sections, as opposed to having an easy takeoff and lining up a barrel, or threading one that's easy off the drop. When you're dropping really hard off the initial drop and barrel, I think that's where the high-scoring potential is.

One interesting issue at Teahupo'o is that there's the judges in the tower and there's the pack in the channel, and both perspectives offer different takes on the wave. I think the tower perspective is truer for depth and takeoff and length of the barrel, which for scoring rides we need to have. But we do have video replay that contains the boat angle. Most of the time you don't need that, but sometimes you'll get waves that spit and the surfer is still in there, they don't come out until after the spit, and we'll look at the replay from the side angle to see what they were doing in the barrel, whether they were riding the foamball. We can't let it affect our scoring too much because we need to be true to what we're seeing, but we do take into account the water angle – it's one of the only events where we have that available.

PIC: KIRSTEN/ASP

JUDGING IS A LITTLE BIT OF YOUR EMOTION BECAUSE YOU'RE JUDGING OFF YOUR FEEL OF A RIDE. BUT YOU DEFINITELY HAVE TO HOLD IT BACK AND NOT GET OVEREXCITED

When it's 8-10 feet there's a tremendous emotional component involved. The waves are hitting the reef with sledgehammer power, you can feel the waves hitting the tower, and you can't help but put yourself in the place of the surfer. It's important to understand this as part of the process. Judging is a little bit of your emotion because you're judging off your feel of a ride. But you definitely have to hold it back and not get overexcited or be in their moment too much. If you start getting too involved in their situations and how heavy the waves are and what's going on, then maybe you're not focusing on the job at hand, which is comparing all the waves within that heat.

Former head judge Perry Hatchett used to say that "chicken skin" was a big part of a 10-point ride. That's interesting for me. For some reason I don't get chicken skin. I know when it's a 10, but I've thrown heaps of 10s and not had chicken skin. I don't know if it's my physical makeup or whatever. But you know, the guys will be like "Look at my chicken skin!" and I'll be like, "Dammit! Where's *my* chicken skin!" ∎

THE LURKER

Event winner **Kelly Slater** reflects on tactics, challenges and passions.

I was the lurker here. I never felt like I was the standout guy. I was getting my waves, winning my heats. Then I felt as I got into the semis and quarters I could throw everything at it. Specially in the final I was a lot more active, I caught a lot of different waves. I was trying to wait for big ones, but also trying to sneak in and get those runners and the wedgy inside west bowls, trying to utilise every option, trying to cover all bases, not take too many chances early and get cleaned up.

I had a really bizarre competitive start to the day. I just was off this morning. Fifteen minutes before my heat I realised I'd left my wetsuit at home. I like surfing in the suit because I never get chilly at all. It's a six-minute jetski ride either way, so we thought might be able to get it back here in time. Somebody went and got it and on the way back they dropped it in the water, that was another minute. When they got back there was a minute and 30 seconds until the heat started, I threw my wetsuit on and grabbed my jersey, I'm 30 seconds late. I'm just not in sync. Then I broke my board, then I had a six-footer unload right in front of me. And I couldn't go under it, there was nothing I could do, it just killed me. I was in the lagoon. I got on the sled. I grinded my fins on the reef getting into the lagoon. I was like "What else can happen right now??" I went back out and thought well I guess all the bad stuff's happened, and Wilko didn't even have a score yet.

In the final Owen didn't blink. It doesn't seem to me he's intimidated by anybody or any situation. He likes big waves, he likes barrels, he likes beachbreaks, he likes onshore winds, throw anything at him he's good at it. He just goes toe-to-toe with anybody or anything, backside or frontside. I just knew I had to go surf my own heat and not worry about him too much. It looked like he was going to wait for the big ones so he was almost like eliminating those smaller ones from his repertoire. So I thought, I'll get those medium ones on the inside ledge when he's waiting with priority, I might score a couple of eights or nines, then if he doesn't get in sync and get those 9.7s he's been getting, then I get priority, I can wait for that big one.

I missed the event before this one (Jeffreys Bay) and I think subconsciously I was thinking "I wish I was there!" I actually thought I was gonna get to that contest. I was literally on the way to the airport when they called it on and I went "Dammit! I missed it!" But that probably got me focused for this in some way.

PIC: GRAMBEAU

> I DON'T KNOW HOW MY GIRLFRIEND DEALS WITH IT. I THINK IT'S HARDER FOR HER. SHE'S LIKE "YOU'RE GOING *WHERE* TONIGHT?"

I don't feel age. Baldness, getting old … I'm near 40, whatever, I don't feel it, I don't make choices based on it. I think you can keep getting better – for real, demonstrably, not just in your head or whatever. Look at martial artists. You have to wait to get your red belt – you don't get it until you're old. They don't give it to you when you're 17, or 25. Really the competitive side is the least interesting part of it for me. But contests can be a test, and I like testing myself, seeing that I can surf as well as these guys. Once I stop feeling like I want to do that, I'll know it's time to step back.

I get up every morning and check the swell maps; I still love to do that. I think I'm going to Central America next, just to get this swell.

I don't know how my girlfriend deals with it. I think it's harder for her. She's like "You're going WHERE tonight?" But… it's what I love to do and obviously at some point I'll have a proper home and family and kids and stuff and I'm not going to be able to do that then, so I'm gonna do it while I can. ∎

THE CHALLENGER

Runner-up **Owen Wright** on wins, losses and inspiration.

This event had the best waves I've ever surfed in an event and the most challenging for sure. I don't know what it looked like from outside, but I was working hard to get things right here. Head down, bum up, working hard. But I think if you weren't working hard at this event those waves would knock you right off anyway.

For me I've been trying to make big changes to how I compete for a long time. I've never been such a good loser. I think learning to lose is definitely something that's such a huge issue. When I first made the tour I came off the juniors and I was winning a lot of events at that level. Then I came on the tour and had a few knockbacks. Last year I had a few up and down results, a few losses that were hard to take. Then this year I had a particularly painful loss against Adriano in Brazil. That was hilarious. Everybody was reminding me about it. For the next three weeks I was at home and I went down the south coast and I had little grommies coming up to me and be like: "I saw you just do the SICKEST floater!" It was just hilarious. I came fifth, so while it wasn't a bad result overall, it was a tough loss in that heat.

But it's always gonna be for the better because I always want to learn from it. It always seems to make me go harder, and I'm trying to improve. I'm starting to feel it now, this one's definitely a confidence boost and I'll try to roll it into some more events.

To me, that final, I didn't feel like I made many mistakes. I've had a few heats with Kelly now, and he's been such an inspiration to me, he definitely brings out the best in me. When we're out in heats he does his thing and I do mine and I see how it pans out. Like at Lowers last year we had two heats, I kept doing my thing and one heat turned out in my favour and then the quarterfinal I went left and he got me there. It's one of those things. You can't stop Kelly doing his thing. I was out there to choose my waves and he was out there to choose

his. I'm always watching him.

I loved that I sucked him into a wave late in the final. It was a good wave and it was definitely worthy. He had priority and I needed the score, so he did what he had to do on that wave and you never know what might have happened if he didn't. I paddled and sucked him in and he tried to pull back and got sucked over the falls. I stood up watching him and did a big pump and just got past him, dove under and got back out. There was two minutes left in the heat and it was there for the taking. Swell didn't come, but still…

But it was a really fun heat, and talking to him after it finished

> I'VE NEVER BEEN SUCH A GOOD LOSER. I THINK LEARNING TO LOSE IS DEFINITELY SOMETHING THAT'S SUCH A HUGE ISSUE.

it was the same, he was just stoked to be out there having a heat with me, because it was just surfing, there wasn't anything else to it. There's something he's got that not many other guys have got. He's been the man for a long time now.

I'm happy with a final and stoked to learn from it and pick it to pieces. This has been a huge learning experience for me, so thanks to my friends and family for helping me get here. I take my hat off to my family, they've been so supportive. The phone gets lit up every time I make a heat, so it's pretty good to come back to.

They're not travelling with me as much this year but for sure they're gonna pop up in places around the world, there's too many of 'em. Mikey's gonna be in France, I know he'll be there and most probably my brother Tim because he's filming a lot. I always love having my dad around at events, he's too funny to watch, he's always the first guy out there surfing and taking waves off the other boys, so maybe it works out well for me that way! ■

THE BIG DAY OUT

Laurie Towner on Code Red.

It didn't really start all that well. I go to Tahiti for the trials and for once we don't have any waves. I have a shocker and get knocked out. I fly out the day the 'CT guys start turning up. It's the same day everyone sees the swell on the forecast pop up. So I hang out at home for a week, the phone rings off the hook, and I jump back on a plane and get back over there.

It's Saturday. I wake up in the dark and walk downstairs and Dyl's already up getting his stuff ready. I run out the front and had a look and first thing I see is the biggest barrel I've ever seen out there. It's a grey, stormy, big ocean-looking day.

Where we stay, at Mommy and Poppy's, we look from the jetty across the channel straight into the eyeball of the wave. You can tell from what's going on in the channel what's going on out the back. Today the jetty's almost getting taken away. There are stationary waves in the channel, rapids as gnarly as I've seen there.

We shoot out in a boat to check it out. First thing I see is some maniac bodyboarder eat shit. He gets pumped on a 15-footer and washed into the lagoon. A lot of the waves are barrelling perfectly, but at the end they just fold down on themselves. I'm amped, thinking "Let's give this a crack", but also aware that it's as nuts and as scary as it gets. It looks dangerous.

We head back in to get ready. We think we've got a ski sorted, but the crew are saying the Government isn't allowing our skis in the water 'cos of the Code Red. They won't let us use any of our stuff. We're freaking. We can see guys starting to tow in the distance. You don't want to be sitting around waiting and watching 'cos the more you watch the more nervous you get. Then finally we sort it out with

some black tape over the branding and we head out.

We get out there and there's hundreds of people in the channel, but there's no-one in the lineup! At this stage we don't know that Raimana's told people to stop because everyone was just getting nailed. The end was just closing out. Some of the heaviest wipeouts went down in the morning.

We watch for a while and see two decent ones, semi-rideable. So we fang out the back without talking to anyone. I tap Dylan on the shoulder and say "Do you wanna go first?" and he looks back at at me and says "Do YOU wanna go first?" So I just go "Fuck it" and get

PIC: DAWE

> ONCE YOU'VE GOT THE ROPE YOUR NERVES RELAX A BIT. BUT WHEN YOU'RE ON THE SKI YOU START TO GET NERVOUS AGAIN.

straight into it and get two good ones straight off the bat. And from there all the skis come back out and it's all on.

As the day goes on it feels like it gets bigger, but it gets cleaner, and the tide gets better. There are still some evil waves, but some of them are as good as it gets. Some of the shit I see is so incredible and there's so much happening I kinda can't take it in or remember it.

There aren't just one or two amazing rides, there's 20. And 20 all-time wipeouts too.

When we're towing, we'll catch a couple and swap over when we've had a good one. Once you've got the rope your nerves relax a bit. But when you're on the ski you start to get nervous again.

I get about seven waves, fall on three or four of 'em so it's a 50/50 success rate. I get flogged, but don't slam the bottom, which is the scariest thing for everyone out there. You're not worried about being held under, you're more worried about slamming or knocking yourself out. That's the scariest thing.

One wipeout was pretty scary. I come out of a barrel and get sucked over and get held under for so long. I've got my vest on, but it's not letting me back to the surface. I'm doing flips and whatever for ages. Once it's pushed me in, I can feel it drawing me back into the zone, like I'm caught in the draw as it's draining off the reef back into the next wave. I think I'm in serious trouble. And I still can't break the surface. Then I finally I pop up and I'm fully in the lagoon! It's like "Yes! I'm saved, I'm safe, I'm in the lagoon!"

ME AND DYL HAVE GOT A GOOD THING HAPPENING. WE'VE SURFED A LOT OF GOOD SWELLS TOGETHER.

PIC: FRIEDEN

The scariest thing about wipeouts in those waves is when you're in the lip and you're going down to the reef. Once you know you're not hitting the reef with force it doesn't matter how long you're under for. Touch wood it's a good day and I don't get hurt.

Far as driving the ski goes, everyone's got their own techniques. It starts from a hundred metres out: You're right in front of the lump, then on top of the swell, and right at the last minute it seems to catch up with you and you basically drive towards the boats off the back of the wave. You keep that constant speed and the surfer lets go when he's ready. They'll let go before you think they do most of the time. It's quite an easy wave to tow, the boats in the channel give you the lineup perfectly.

I follow right behind the wave, right behind where it's exploding, so your wake doesn't mess up the wave behind. You hang behind the wave and look at the boats' reaction to see if he's gone down or not. If everyone points you know he's gone down. I just wait, then fang in to get to 'em before the next wave , grab 'em and get 'em on the ski, 'cos a lot of the times the gnarliest wipeouts are gonna be the next wave cleaning 'em up. If you're in the wrong spot there it could be all over. So you grab 'em and fang into the lagoon where you're safe.

Me and Dyl have got a good thing happening. We've surfed a lot of good swells together. He shapes my boards and we've been good friend from the start of my surfing career. He's always been there. We're comfortable towing together, especially at Teahupo'o 'cos he's been there so many times and knows it really well. Dyl's so on to it, he knows what he's doing.

Today we're out there from 9.00am to 3.00pm going hard. There's 10 tow teams out there so you gotta wait your turn and try to pick the right waves. After six hours we come in and start drinking beers on the deck. We're sitting there, looking straight into the eye of the wave, wondering if we should have stayed out longer. Dyl's going "Fuck, we should get some more." and I'm like "Nah, let's just quit, we had a good run, let's not get hurt." It's weird though, sitting watching, 'cos some of the better waves of the day come through that arvo.

We hang around for the rest of the comp. We don't feel like surfing so we just cruise. We watch the contest online. It's too hot to sit in a boat in the sun if you're not gonna surf.

The day after the contest I don't want to surf at all, I'm done for a month. But we're sitting out on the deck and Chopes is looking pretty good, so me and Dyl head out. It's as perfect as it gets, four foot and not a soul out! It's one of the funnest surfs I've ever had out there. Fifty barrels in an hour. Me and Dyl surf for ages. We didn't intend to surf, but how can you not? ∎

EVENT

WITH THANKS TO THE
FAMILIES OF TEAHUPO'O
WHO WELCOME THE WORLD INTO THEIR HOME

Emma and Fritz, Mummy and Poppy Maoni, Benny B, Hering and Nellina Parker,
Eric and Jacueline Plantier, Tevia Rochett, Julia and Michel, Lewis Parker, Teuira Faatauira,
Charles, Serge Parker, Didier and Sidonie, Maria Parker, The Osmond Family, George, Stanley,
Ato Aldophe, Maggie, Alexi, Vetos, Heiani & Celina, Dorres, The Vague Blue, Elwis, Heubert,
The Doom Family, Florence, Lovina, Ginette, Snack Teahupoo, Mareva, The Peva Family,
The Nelson Family, Hira, Pension Cheyene.

WITH THANKS TO THE
TAHITIAN WATER PATROL
FOR THEIR SKILL AND SERVICE

Viri Teiva, Arsene Harehoe, Moana David, Vetea "Poto" David, Honoura Maono, Alvino Manutahi, Patrice Chanzy,
Didier Tin Hin, Georges Buchin, Thierry Domenech, Erich Teihotu, Lucien Raio, Narii Mati.

WITH THANKS TO THE
LOCAL CREW
FOR THEIR HARD WORK

Chris O'Callaghan, Simon Thornton, Bruno Bosman and Jean-Pierre Combescure,
Pascal Luciani, Phillip Klima and the Tahitian Federation de Surf.

WITH THANKS TO THE
DIGNITARIES AND INSTITUTIONS
FOR FACILITATING THIS EVENT

PRESIDENT OF THE GOVERNMENT IN CHARGE OF TOURISM: Oscar Manutahi Temaru // MINISTER OF SPORT: Tauhiti Nena
IJSPF (INSTITUT OF YOUTH AND SPORTS OF FRENCH POLYNESIA): Tonio Arai // GIE TAHITI TOURISM: Teva Janicaud
MAYOR OF TAIARAPU OUEST: Clarrentz Vernaudon // MAYOR OF TEAHUPO'O: Marcelle Holozet

WITH THANKS TO THE
LOCAL PARTNERS
FOR MAKING THIS HAPPEN

OPT // Mana // Vini – Tikiphone // SOPADEP // Hertz // Brasserie de Tahiti // Tahiti Tourism

WITH THANKS TO THE
GLOBAL PARTNERS
FOR MAKING THIS HAPPEN

Air Tahiti Nui – Mark Hutchinson, Craig Lee (In Loving memory) // Sony // Sony Ericsson // Monster Energy Drink // VonZipper // Nixon //
ASL // Surfline // Fuel TV Australia // Universal Music Group // Channel V // Honda

WITH THANKS TO THE
WEBCAST TEAM
FOR THE 20-HOUR DAYS

Stirling Howland, Joel Medeiros, Alex Couta E Silva, Matthew Cleary, Lyle Fielmich, Zander van Oldenborgh, Michael Herring, Nimai Strickland, John Gordon, Kendall O'Brien, Jamie Brooks, Dwayne Fetch, Lachlan Munday, Miriam Torres, Aaron Blake, Mark Occhilupo, Sean Doherty, Paul Daniel, Asher King, Angela Rae, Barry Sutherland, Dwayne Fetch, Luke Egan, Joe Turpel, Greg Tomlinson, Adam Repogle, Jeff Doner.

WITH THANKS TO
ALL INVOLVED
AND APOLOGIES FOR ANY OMISSIONS

Gordon Merchant
Derek O'Neill
Shannan North
Mike Savage
Andrew Flitton
Mick Talbot
Graham Stapleberg
Reid Pinder
Scott Wallace
Brenden Margieson
Steve Robertson
John Mossop

Julian Blanchard
Steph Hendrickson
Marlene Wills
Woody Sedgman
Chris Heffner
Jason Jackson
Billabong Aust
Marketing Department
Billabong Australia
Billabong Europe
Billabong USA
Billabong Brazil

David Wood
Andrew Valder
The Living End
Colbie Caillat
Billabong Print Dept
Billabong Finance team
ASP International
Renato Hickel
Dave Prodan
Richie Porta
Pritamo Ahrendt
Royce Leu

Luke White
Luke Jeffrey
Reid Pinder
Sam Carrier
Alexandra Traisnel
Johnno & Eclipse crew
Brian Bielmann
Mike Perry
OBM International
Bow Edwards
Sasha Stocker
Maurice Wakeling

Ben Prosser
Adrian Dent
Daniel Haley
Paul Scott
James Marr
Jonathon Jenkins
Storm Wood
Vasco Coves
Micah Leroy
David Ellis
Adrian Hunter
Paul Fischer

Graham Short
Chris Prosser
Gavin Clark
Jaclyn Kate McGibbony
Mary Showstark
Roslyn Kelly
Nick Carroll
Nick Pollet
Russ Jackson
Steve Shearer
Billabong Management
The Board of Directors

BOOK

WITH THANKS TO
THE PHOTOGRAPHERS
FOR KEEN EYES

TIM **McKENNA** HILTON **DAWE** TED **GRAMBEAU** BEN **THOUARD** PAT **STACY** PETE **FRIEDEN** STEVE **ROBERTSON** CHRIS **BURKARD**

WITH THANKS TO
THE CONTRIBUTORS
FOR SHARING

SEAN **COLLINS** MICK **TALBOT** DR PAUL **FISCHER** PRITAMO **AHRENDT** KELLY **SLATER** OWEN **WRIGHT** LAURIE **TOWNER**

WITH THANKS TO
THE CREW AT BILLABONG
FOR A SWEET COLLABORATION

ANDREW **FLITTON** STEPH **HENDRICKSON** JAMIE **BROOKS** ROYCEY **LEU** BOW **EDWARDS** MICK **TALBOT** MICHAEL **CALVINO** BRENDEN **MARGIESON** KENDALL **O'BRIEN**

A
MORRISON MEDIA
PUBLICATION

OWNER FOUNDER	PROJECT PUBLISHER	PRODUCTION MANAGER	DIGITAL PREPRESS	PRINTED BY
PETER **MORRISON**	CRAIG **SIMS**	JOHN **HARLAND**	GLEN **MORRISON**	FAST PROOF **PRESS**

WRITER + MENTOR	EDITOR + DESIGNER
NICK **CARROLL**	GRA **MURDOCH**

RAIMANA
VAN
BASTOLAER

SEQUENCE
CONTINUES →

SEQUENCE
CONTINUES →

SEQUENCE
CONTINUES →

"

Every year I look forward to everyone visiting.

We're all proud to have people from here and overseas be amazed by this place.

From two feet to 25 feet, as far as the vibe goes, there's no place like it in the world.

When everyone is gone, it's a ghost town.

We miss people. I miss my friends, but it's how it is.

This day (a week after finals day) was amazing. I got out there early and just a few guys were out. I caught a few waves, but everyone started to leave.

I ended up surfing it by myself.

So I called up John & Nathan Florence, Albee Layer and Taumata and they came surfing with me.

It was incredible. No-one got hurt, and they all went home smiling.

Thank you Teahupo'o!

"

RAIMANA
VAN
BASTOLAER

1 Blue "Space Case" Container x1 // 2 Internal Communication Units x38 // 3 Wet Bags (For walkie talkies) x38 // 4 Spare Parts x20 // 5 Blue "Space Case" Container x1 // 6 Battery Charger units x8 // 7 Blue "Space Case" container x1 // 8 Assorted Digital TV Cables x30 // 9 Black Pelican Case x1 // 10 Siemens Modem Router x1 // 11 Siemens Modem Router x1 // 12 D-Link Modem Router x1 // 13 D-Link Modem Router x1 // 14 D-Link Modem Router x1 // 15 D-Link Modem Router x1 // 16 D-Link Modem Router x1 // 17 D-Link Modem Router x1 // 18 D-Link Modem Router x1 // 19 Smart View Video Splitter x1 // 20 Philmore Step Up/Down Transformer x1 // 21 Blue Nylex Storage Container x1 // 22 Assorted Web Cables x25 // 23 Blue Nylex Storage Container x1 // 24 Assorted Web Cables x30 // 25 Blue Nylex Storage Container x1 // 26 Peter Martin Sales Transformer x1 // 27 Blue Nylex Storage Container x1 // 28 Nikko UPS x1 // 29 Blue Nylex Storage Container x1 // 30 Nikko UPS x1 // 31 Red Road Case x1 // 32 Phillips Monitor Screen x1 // 33 ViewSonic Flat Screen Monitor x2 // 34 Red Road Case x1 // 35 Phillips Monitor Screens x2 // 36 Phillips Monitor Screens x2 // 37 Blue Space Case x1 // 38 Extension leads x23 // 39 Blue Nylex Storage Container x1 // 40 European Power Boards x18 // 41 Black Storage container x1 // 42 French/USA Extension Leads x16 // 43 Grey space case x1 // 44 Extension leads x6 // 45 Safety Switches x2 // 46 Power Boards x6 // 47 Black Storage container x1 // 48 Arlec Spot Lights x6 // 49 Phillips Spotlight x1 // 50 White Nylex Container x1 // 51 Power Boards x20 // 52 White Nylex Container x1 // 53 Safety Switches x10 // 54 Extension leads x5 // 55 Waterproof Safety Boxes x2 // 56 Black Storage container x1 // 57 Lrg Extension Leads x2 // 58 Lrg Powerboards x3 // 59 Green Storage Container x1 // 60 Power Adaptors x40 // 61 Switch board x1 // 62 Blue Nylex Storage Container x1 // 63 Tub Screws, Nails x1 // 64 Packets Cable Ties x7 // 65 Grommet repair kit x1 // 66 Rolls Tape x14 // 67 Tape Guns x2 // 68 Blue Nylex Storage Container x1 // 69 Makita Drill x1 // 70 Bosch Drill x1 // 71 Small tub assorted drill fittings x1 // 72 Staple Gun x1 // 73 Metal Box x1 // 74 Bolt Cutters x1 // 75 Handsaws x2 // 76 Hacksaws x2 // 77 Slide hammer x1 // 78 corking gun x1 // 79 Sledge-hammers x2 // 80 Level x1 // 81 G Clamps x2 // 82 Torch x1 // 83 Goggles x1 // 84 5m wire x1 // 85 Small box compressor parts x1 // 86 Hammers x2 // 87 Red Ferno Medical Bag x1 // 88 Black Pelican Case Medical x1 // 89 Metal Medical Box x1 // 90 Red Kathmandu Medical Bag x1 // 91 Metal Oxy Resuscitator x1 // 92 Big Red Esky x1 // 93 Billabong Tablecloths x6 // 94 Oxy Bottles x4 // 95 Big Red Esky x1 // 96 Silk Flags x6 // 97 Wormald Extinguishers x3 // 98 Big Red Esky x1 // 99 Haier TV Monitor Screen x1 // 100 15m Mesh Banners x2 // 101 Blue Containers for Stationery x3 // 102 Black Nylex Container x1 // 103 Extension lead cord only/ Spares x4 // 104 White Nylex Container x1 // 105 Monitor Leads/Electrical Parts x15 // 106 Grey Tool Box x1 // 107 Screwdrivers x9 // 108 Scissors x1 // 109 Hammer x1 // 110 Tape measure x1 // 111 Pliers x1 // 112 Cutters x4 // 113 Spanners set x1 // 114 Allen Key set x1 // 115 Mine Level x1 // 116 Stanley Knives x3 // 117 Green Nylex Container x1 // 118 Assorted rags x1 // 119 500ml Metho x1 // 120 500ml Bleach x1 // 121 500ml Mineral Turpentine x1 // 122 Roll paper towel x1 // 123 1litre Washing detergent x1 // 124 750ml Disinfectant x1 // 125 Yamaha 25 HP Outboards x3 // 126 Yamaha 25HP Outboards x2 // 127 Mercury 25HP Outboard x1 // 128 Outboard trolleys x6 // 129 Outboard fuel containers x5 // 130 Ambulance Backpack medical x1 // 131 Metal Box x1 // 132 Marine (Wharf) float connections x20 // 133 Wheelie Bins x1 // 134 Marker Buoys x6 // 135 Set Assorted ropes x1 // 136 Anchors x3 // 137 Small Marker Buoys x2 // 138 Large Marker Buoys x3 // 139 Tubs of Chain x3 // 140 Life Jackets x5 // 141 Blue Nylex Container x1 // 142 Spark Plugs x8 //

CHECKLIST
CONTAINER ONE
BILL4001272